JN296843

英語総合教材

Joseph Shaules

Juri Abe

Different Realities
Adventures in Intercultural Communication

異文化間コミュニケーション―己を知る、相手を知る―

NAN'UN-DO
03-3268-2311

Different Realities
Adventures in Intercultural Communication

Copyright © 1997

by

Joseph Shaules
Juri Abe

**ENGLISH PROGRAM RIKKYO UNIVERSITY
CENTER FOR GENERAL CURRICULUM DEVELOPMENT**

All Rights Reserved

No part of this book may be reproduced in any form without written permission from the authors and Nan'un-do Co., Ltd.

このテキストの音声を無料で視聴（ストリーミング）・ダウンロードできます。自習用音声としてご活用ください。
以下のサイトにアクセスしてテキスト番号で検索してください。

https://nanun-do.com　テキスト番号 [511024]

※ 無線 LAN（WiFi）に接続してのご利用を推奨いたします。
※ 音声ダウンロードは Zip ファイルでの提供になります。
　お使いの機器によっては別途ソフトウェア（アプリケーション）の導入が必要となります。

音声ファイル
無料 DL
のご案内

※ Different Realities 音声ダウンロードページは以下の QR コードからもご利用になれます。

はじめに

　外国の人々とのコミュニケーションが円滑にゆかないのは、多くは言葉の違いであると私たちは考えやすい。もちろんお互いの言葉が通じなければ、充分な意思の疎通ははかれないが、身ぶりや手振りあるいは絵を描いたりして、なんらかの意志を伝えることはできる。異なる文化背景を持つ人々との意志の相互伝達は、言葉による（バーバル）コミュニケーション、言葉によらない（ノンバーバル）コミュニケーション、そしてそれらコミュニケーションの土台、枠組み、指針となっている、それぞれの文化が内包する価値観、思想・信条、伝統、美意識のすべてを含む。

　異文化間コミュニケーションの学習は、国際化の進む世界でより重要性を増している。それは単に貿易やビジネス機会の拡充といった経済志向性にのみともなうものではなく、南北問題が如実にしめす資源、富の甚だしい不均衡、偏在、自民族中心主義（エスノセントリズム）から生じる地域紛争を乗り越え、人類が有限の地球資源を賢明に活用しながら、より平和に生きてゆける地球規模の共生社会を作り出してゆくのに、欠くことのできない視座を私たちに提供するからである。

　私たちと異質な人々、また事象との接触、その理解、そして受容は、私たちが囚われている既成の考えを揺さぶり、意識の変革を促し、相対的なものの見方に導いてくれる。またこれこそが、学びとしての「異文化間コミュニケーション」の目指すべきところである。

　筆者は、この学びを言語教育の中で行うことができたらと考えた。もとより言語は、人の生活と思考に深く根ざし、文化の枠組みの中で育まれてきたものだ。文化学習は言語学習への確実な動機づけともなる。英語教育における「異文化教育」の重要性が謳われて久しいが、なかなか実効性のあるプログラムが登場しない。それは日本が、単一民族社会ではないにしろ、多文化社会の歴史の長い欧米や他のアジア諸国と比べて文化多様性に乏しく、それゆえ多様性、エスニシティーに対する感覚が鈍く、かつ許容度の低い風土であることと、無縁ではないだろう。学びを通じての個々の意識の変革—consciousness raising の大切さがここにもある。

　このテキストの各章は、異文化コミュニケーションにおける重要概念を中心にまとめられている。各章は、問題提起となる lead-in story, それを補強する reading passage が一つのまとまりをなし、内容理解を確認するための Focus on Content, 問題意識を広げるCulture Quiz, consciousness raisingを目的としたActivitiesという構成になっている。この教科書が少しでも学習者の相対的世界観の獲得につながることを願う。

　このテキストはもともと、立教大学全学共通カリキュラム英語教育科目の「言語文化コース」のために書かれた。言語教育を媒体とした「異文化教育」という私たちの新しい試みを全学的に実施するにあたっては、その準備期間も含めれば、実に6年有余に渡って全学的な議論を行ってきた。その間、一貫して私たちを理解、支援してくださった全学共通カリキュラム運営センター準備委員会委員長塚田理、押見輝男の両先生、全学共通カリキュラム運営センター現部長所一彦、前部長寺崎昌男の両先生、さらには、各学部代表の運営委員の先生方に厚くお礼申し上げる。また立教大学の言語教育改革を中心的に担った英語教育研究室の仲間たち—原川恭一、実松克義、渡辺信二、白石典義、鳥飼慎一郎、鳥飼玖美子、野田研一、三浦雅弘、マーク・カプリオ、ポール・カニングハム各氏に謝辞を述べたい。このテキストの完成は、彼らの有用なコメント、提案そしてモラル・サポートに負うところが大きい。ランゲージセンターの佐々木由美、根橋玲子両氏からは、このテキストを実際に試用してもらい、有効なフィードバックを頂いた。北海学園大学の桂晴子氏にもお礼申し上げる。もちろん、あり得るすべての過誤は筆者の責任である。

1997年8月15日

　　　　　　　　　　　　　　　　　　　　　　　　阿部　珠理
　　　　　　　　　　　　　　　　　　　　　　　　ジョセフ・ショールズ

Table of Contents

はしがき iii

1. **Culture and Identity** 1
   文化ってなに？

2. **Hidden Culture** 8
   見えない文化が、私たちの判断を左右する

3. **Stereotypes** 15
   思いこみが、コミュニケーションを妨げる

4. **Words, Words, Words** 23
   言葉の違いが生むコミュニケーション・ギャップ

5. **Communication Without Words** 31
   ノンバーバル・コミュニケーション―身体は話す

6. **Diversity** 39
   ひとつの国には、一つの文化しかない？　様々な文化の共存

7. **Perception** 47
   緑は青？　ピンクは桃色？　文化によって異なる見方

8. **Communication Styles (1)** 56
   「沈黙」もコミュニケーションのシグナル

9. **Communication Styles (2)** 63
   腹芸ってどんな芸？―語る文化、語らぬ文化

10. **Values** 71
    行動の規範となる価値観は文化によって様々

11. **Deep Culture (Beliefs and Values)** 79
    文化を支える思想・信条―個人主義・集団主義

12. **Culture Shock** 87
    カルチャー・ショックから学ぶこと

Chapter 1
Culture and Identity

"They're identical twins. They share all their jeans."

Genes and Jeans

Until recently I've always thought of Jamie as my best friend, even though he is my brother. We're identical twins and grew up sharing everything. When we were kids we loved wearing matching Levis and striped shirts. We used to play practical jokes on our teachers or even relatives, pretending to be each other, or finishing each other's sentences.

Even our friends had trouble telling us apart. When we were 16, a girl that Jamie had met at the beach one day stopped me on the street, thinking I was him. I talked to her and we went to play video games together, but she never knew I wasn't Jamie. It was almost easier than explaining that I was actually his brother. I got her phone number for him and they ended up going on a few dates—but she never found out the truth.

Jamie and I started having trouble last year when he went to France for a study abroad program. Last month he came back after a year in Paris, but he had changed. Now he talks about France and has this negative attitude about America. He says he simply had his eyes opened to the outside world. He talks about how American food is too greasy, and how Hollywood movies are childish. He dresses differently—says he never knew what style was before. He learned about wine, and talks about how children in France drink it with dinner and what an art it is to make it. I think that's fine for people in France, but he is in Indiana now.

I know that Hollywood has its faults and I'm sure French wine is great, but somehow his attitude bothers me. He seems to be a different person. Maybe I'm jealous. Or maybe I'm sad because we always shared everything and I've unconsciously counted on him in ways I didn't realize.

It's made me think about who I am, and how my background has shaped me. I'm Jamie's brother because of biology, but I'm American because I was raised here. Even though we share our genes, we now have different experiences, and so we may not always share our jeans.

1-3   This story is about trouble in Jamie's relationship with his brother. The cause is Jamie's experience in France and how that has changed him. The subject of this book is similar—how to improve our relationships and our communication with people who are different from us.

This first chapter looks at the connection between culture and identity. Our relationships and communication style with others depend not only on personality, but also on our culture. Jamie and his brother had trouble because of what Jamie learned in France. There was a conflict between two cultures.

Many people think of culture as things like Kabuki or Ikebana. This book looks at **culture** more broadly as the things that members of a group share in common. Using this definition, culture includes everything from language and customs to values and communication styles. We can talk about Japanese values or communication style and compare them with Chinese or Turkish values and communication styles, for example. Or, we can talk about comparing Kansai culture with Kanto culture, or look at male-female communication differences.

> Culture includes everything from language and customs to values and communication styles.

Intercultural communication focuses on the things that members of a group share, like values and communication styles. Of course there is individual difference, but it exists within a shared framework of expectations and ideas about how to act and get along. The actions and attitudes of people from other cultures are often misinterpreted if their cultural point of view is not understood and respected. This contributes to national and international conflict: wars, trade friction, discrimination against certain members of society, ethnic rivalry, etc. On the personal level it can create negative stereotypes, cause an international marriage to fail, make a homestay student miserable, or cause a manager abroad to do his job poorly.

The purpose of studying intercultural communication is to help students be ready for the challenges of dealing with a wide range of people. The first step in doing this is to look at how our culture creates and shapes our identity. As we understand more clearly what it means to say "I am Japanese" (if one is Japanese), it becomes easier to appreciate someone who is different.

Most importantly, our **cultural identity** is learned. Japanese bow, take off shoes before entering a building, eat with chopsticks, value cooperation and use honorific language because they learn to. Returnees who have trouble adjusting to Japanese society remind us how much identity is related to what we learn from our experiences.

The process of gaining our identity from our culture is called

socialization. This involves learning how to look at the world and get along with others. American children learn to be American by how they are raised, with emphasis on things like the importance of independence. For example, American children sleep separately from their parents at a very young age. Japanese children learn Japanese culture in the same way. For example, when a child is told "*Hito ga miteru kara yamenasai!*" she or he learns the importance of paying close attention to the people around one. In a similar way children all over the world learn to honor their elders, say, or eat with their fingers, cross on the green light, use money, avoid certain plants, and so on.

> The process of gaining our identity from our culture is called **socialization**.

In Japan, the feeling that Japanese are very similar to each other and very different from non-Japanese is quite strong. This idea is partly true and partly false. Most cultures interact with and are influenced by other cultures. Japan's culture shares important common roots with Korea and China, and has recently been greatly influenced by western culture, especially that of the U.S. Also, there are many qualities that all cultures share in common.

There is no way to say any culture is more unique than any other. We can only compare one culture relative to another. Many North Americans may have trouble understanding the Japanese values of *mentsu* or *giri*, for example, but for Koreans or Chinese it is easier. We also have to remember that not all Japanese are the same. Different regions and social groups within Japan also have their own distinct cultures. Appreciating this is also part of the study of intercultural communication. There are many important social issues related to understanding these cultures within a culture. They include the status of ethnic Koreans in Japan, integrating the disabled into society, and the recognition of the cultural traditions of the Ainu and Okinawa.

> We also have to remember that not all Japanese are the same.

Relating well to people from other cultures requires a balance between the knowledge that all humans share certain qualities, and the understanding that differences between cultures are very important and need to be understood and respected. That can be difficult, as Jamie's brother is finding out, but can also be extremely rewarding as we get a fresh perspective on life, and maybe even learn about the art of making wine.

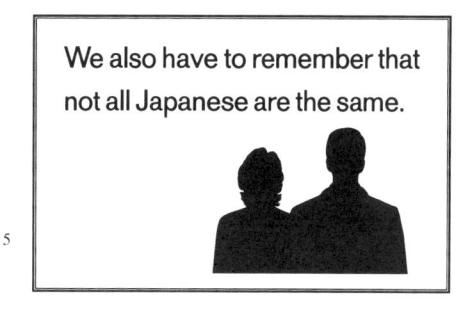

Did you know?

Japan is often described as a collectivist, or group-oriented culture, but many other cultures are too. Below is a ranking of 40 different countries, from most group-oriented—Venezuela—to most individualistic—the United States.

1 - **Venezuela**	11 - Portugal	21 - Spain	31 - Sweden
2 - Colombia	12 - Mexico	22 - Israel	32 - Denmark
3 - Pakistan	13 - Philippines	23 - Austria	33 - Belgium
4 - Peru	14 - Greece	24 - Finland	34 - Italy
5 - Taiwan	15 - Turkey	25 - South Africa	35 - New Zealand
6 - Thailand	16 - Brazil	26 - Germany	36 - Netherlands
7 - Singapore	17 - Iran	27 - Switzerland	37 - Canada
8 - Chile	18 - Argentina	28 - Norway	38 - Great Britain
9 - Hong Kong	**19 - Japan**	29 - Ireland	39 - Australia
10 - Yugoslavia	20 - India	30 - France	**40 - United States**

(source - *Communication Between Cultures*, Samovar and Porter, 2nd edition, Wadsworth)

DIFFERENT REALITIES

Focus on Content

1. Relate the story of Jamie and his brother with the reading passage which follows the story. The title of the story "Genes and Jeans" refers to:
    a. how biology shapes our identity.
    b. how experience shapes us regardless of biology.
    c. how culture is determined by genes.
    d. how humans are similar in spite of shared differences.

2. Based on what you read, what do you think it means to have a "cultural experience"? (This is only hinted at in the text.)
    a. Going to a foreign country.
    b. Changing your lifestyle after discovering a better way to do things.
    c. Being influenced by contact with groups that are different than oneself.
    d. Finding out that your values come from your culture.

3. According to the text, socialization:
    a. teaches children manners.
    b. teaches children how to look at the world.
    c. teaches children values.
    d. all of the above.

4. According to the text:
    a. all cultures are basically the same.
    b. Japanese culture is unrelated to any other culture.
    c. cultures can only be compared with each other.
    d. some cultures are not unique.

5. According to the text, to relate well to people from other cultures, it's important to remember that:
    a. similarities and differences between cultures are both important.
    b. people are basically the same.
    c. all cultures are very different.
    d. Japanese culture is unique.

Culture Quiz

Based on what is written in the text, do you think the following are considered cultural groups?

1. women   yes no
2. people with black skin   yes no
3. short people   yes no
4. deaf people   yes no
5. people from India   yes no
6. people from Osaka   yes no

Activities

1. In order to better understand how our identity affects our communication style, with a partner:

   ★**Act out a scene** at the breakfast table, taking the role of mother and father to compare the communication styles of men and women. Also, try a scene of parent and child. Male students should try playing female roles and vice versa. Can you play the role of someone from a different part of the country, or of a foreigner?

   ★**Evaluate your partners** on how well they were able to make their communication style fit the role they were playing. **Make a list** of the differences you found between the different roles.

2. **Make a cultural profile of yourself:**

   ★**Make a list** of the groups that you belong to. For example: male, young person, student, city person, Japanese, etc.

   ★**Choose three** that are most important to your identity. Imagine being told that you are the opposite of each item. For example, if you are a boy, imagine being told "You seem like a girl"; if "young person" is on your list, imagine being told that you act like an old person, etc. If you dislike being told a certain thing, then that item is important to your identity.

   ★**Compare** your list with someone else and **discuss** whether your particular cultural profile influences your communication style. For example, maybe someone for whom being young is very important doesn't enjoy chatting with older people and uses a lot of popular slang words.

Chapter 2
Hidden Culture

Important parts of culture are hidden.

"Meet any cute girls lately?" 1-5

Kenji is a 3rd year university student. He recently started studying at an English conversation school in Tokyo in order to help his chances of finding a good job after graduation. He is in the school lounge during a coffee break. Kenji's usual teacher is Paul. Paul is 28, from Australia, and has been in Japan only a few months. Kenji likes Paul, but sometimes has trouble answering his questions, like: "So what's new?" or "Have you met any cute girls lately?" On this day, Paul introduces Kenji to a new teacher, Kirk. Kenji is a bit nervous speaking with native speakers although he got good grades in English in high school and is very social and popular among his own friends.

Paul: Oh, Kenji, have you met Kirk? This is Kenji.

Kirk: Hi, how's it going? (Kirk looks Kenji in the eye but Kenji looks away, uncomfortable. Kirk vaguely feels Kenji is weak.)

Kenji: My name is Kenji Okamoto. Nice to meet you. (Kenji didn't answer Kirk's question.)

Kirk: Uh, yeah, nice to meet you too. How's everything going? (Kirk asks again, using casual language, expecting that to create a friendly atmosphere.)

Kenji: Fine, thank you. And you? (Kenji doesn't give information about himself.)

Kirk: Okay, I guess. I'm trying to learn everyone's name. (Kirk talks about himself—wants Kenji to be more personal.)

Kenji: (Pause) Where are you from? (Kenji changes the subject. It seems impersonal to Kirk.)

Kirk: I'm from the U.S.—North Dakota. Do you know where that is? (Kirk doesn't like the conversation too focused on himself. He wants Kenji to talk more.)

Kenji: No. (Pause) (Kenji expects Kirk to control the conversation, so waits.)

Kirk: (Pause) So, how do you like Paul's class? (Kirk waited for Kenji to say more, but he didn't. Kirk is tired of asking questions. He wants an opinion, not a fact.)

Kenji: Uh, it's nice. (Pause) (Kenji isn't sure why he was asked this. Paul has been watching, and tries to help the conversation move along.)

Paul: Kenji's a university student. He looks serious, but actually he's a wild guy with dozens of girlfriends. (Paul feels Kenji is stiff, and wants him to react.)

Kenji: No, it's a joke. (Pause) (Kenji feels Paul doesn't seem like a very serious teacher, but thinks he's cool. He feels that all foreigners are a little wild. He wants to learn more about Paul and Kirk, so he waits.)

Kirk: Well, it's nice meeting you. I'll see you later. (Kirk feels he has been working hard in this conversation, but getting no response.)

Kenji: Okay, good-bye. (Kenji feels off balance because he can't anticipate what Kirk or Paul will say. He feels his English is poor even though he understood everything that was said.)

Soon after that Kenji stopped going to that school. He didn't think deeply about the reason, but told his friends that English was not worth the trouble. A few months later, Paul returned to Australia without finishing his teaching contract. He told Kirk he had come to Japan for a new experience, but was tired of having to be an "entertainer" just to get his students to speak, and of being treated as a "gaijin".

This conversation didn't start a war or create a flood of refugees, but it still represents a failure in intercultural communication. Kenji's goal was to improve his English. Instead, he was nervous and dissatisfied, and stopped going to class. But his problems were not with English itself. He understood what was said to him, and was able to reply, and even to ask questions. Still, he didn't feel the conversation was smooth. In class, he had trouble with questions like "Did you meet any cute girls lately?", but not because he didn't understand what was being said.

Paul said he wanted a new experience in Japan, but he had trouble adjusting. Apparently, he was frustrated with teaching because he had trouble getting students to speak up. Also, we don't know in detail what he meant by being treated as a "gaijin", but in some way his expectations were not met, and he ended up, like Kenji, dissatisfied with interaction with people from another culture.

There is another failure here that is less obvious. Kenji and Paul did not gain in self-awareness. If they reflected on their experiences, they might have realized that they needed to have more cultural flexibility. Kenji was uncomfortable because English-style conversations are different from those in Japanese, and Paul's expectations about his students were based on his experiences in Australia, and didn't fit Japan. Their failure is that they didn't learn about themselves. Their learning stopped and turned into negative feelings.

Kenji may give up on learning about English or English speakers. Maybe it even created negative feelings about foreigners. Paul had a bigger failure than Kenji. He invested time and energy (and money?) coming to Japan, but left with neg-

Hidden Culture: Cultural elements that we don't notice consciously, but rather that we feel intuitively.

ative feelings. He was making an effort in his work, but was frustrated with students' response. He needed to think more deeply about the causes of his frustration. Was he doing some things that might make it more difficult for students to speak up?

Paul didn't like being a "gaijin". He was treated differently than he would have treated a foreign visitor to Australia. If he had paid closer attention, though, it might have been easier to accept that in general, the style of showing hospitality was the problem rather than any bad intentions or unreasonableness on the part of Japanese.

*   *   *

English and Japanese language and culture are different in hidden ways. At least part of Kenji's problems was related to the difference in flow between conversations in English and those in Japanese. One important purpose of the questions Kirk asked Kenji was to encourage Kenji to talk about himself, because this is a common strategy in English for small talk. Japanese small talk is less focused on talking about oneself, and Kenji simply wasn't able to adapt.

Obvious cultural differences—like using chopsticks rather than knife and fork—cause few problems because people know how to approach the task at hand, and can learn efficiently because the goal is clear. Hidden culture, though, like conversation styles, values, feelings about basic things like time, or money, or status, cause infinitely more trouble. These subtle differences are not obvious, and so can be hard to recognize consciously. Instead we feel them. In both Kenji and Paul's case, at least partly because they didn't clearly understand the cause of their feelings, they ended up giving up.

An important skill for dealing with hidden culture is the ability to be

> **Perceptiveness**: The ability to notice a lot about the things around you.

perceptive, to notice a lot about the people and things around you. If Kenji and Paul had been more perceptive, maybe they would both still be at the English school—maybe even talking about whether Kenji had met any "cute girls".

Did you Know? 1-7

When there is a change of speakers in English, there usually isn't more than a three-second pause before the new speaker says something, even if it is only "hmmm..."

Conversations in English are sometimes described as a game of tennis, with the conversation ball being passed back and forth. Japanese conversations are described as a game of bowling, where each speaker takes a turn while others watch and react, until their turn comes around.

Japanese sometimes say Americans are expressive and outgoing, but some Latins consider Americans cold and overly rational.

2 : Hidden Culture

Focus on Content

1. How do you think the authors of this book define a "failure in intercultural communication" in line 2, page 10?
    a. A communication misunderstanding which creates international problems like trade friction or war.
    b. Feeling nervous or uncomfortable when one speaks with someone from a different culture.
    c. Not feeling that a conversation is smooth.
    d. A communicator's goals are not accomplished, because of cultural difference.

2. Based on the ideas in the text, why do you think Paul would ask Kenji if he had met any cute girls?
    a. Paul wants to meet Japanese girls.
    b. Paul is trying to create a friendly atmosphere.
    c. Paul is not a very serious teacher.
    d. Paul thinks Kenji is keeping secrets from him.

3. What is "another failure" mentioned in line 16, page 10?
    a. Kenji didn't figure out English conversation styles.
    b. Kenji didn't study hard enough.
    c. Kenji didn't enjoy English.
    d. Kenji didn't learn more about himself.

4. Why does hidden culture cause more problems than obvious cultural difference?
    a. It's easy to learn how to use chopsticks or a knife and fork.
    b. Because you need to be outgoing all the time.
    c. It can be difficult to identify hidden cultural barriers.
    d. It's necessary to learn quickly because the goal is clear.

5. As a way to deal with the challenges of hidden culture, the text mentions:
    a. having information about the other culture.
    b. having good feelings about the other culture.
    c. having experience with the other culture.
    d. having the ability to notice many things about the other culture.

DIFFERENT REALITIES

Culture Quiz

Every culture has values which are seldom talked about, but which greatly influence how people think and act. Test your intuition about some hidden cultural values in the United States. Circle true (T) if you think the statement represents something commonly felt as true in the U.S.

1. Time is a way to control human behavior. T / F
2. Change is good. T / F
3. One should accept that life is basically controlled by fate. T / F
4. Everyone has the power to make themselves happy. T / F
5. Too much education is bad. T / F
6. Human values are the same everywhere. T / F

Note - People's actions are always influenced by hidden culture. The items listed as true are true to different degrees for different people.

Activities

1. **Answer** the above questions for Japanese culture. Check your answers with others to see if you agree.

2. In pairs or groups, **make a list** of characteristic attitudes of Japanese towards communication. For American culture, a list like that might include items like: conflicts should be resolved through negotiation; being direct is good; informality is friendly; it's good to minimize difference between superiors and subordinates, etc. Compare your list with others.

Chapter 3
Stereotypes

"But I love you . . ."

Dear Mark . . .

The following is a letter written by Tomoe to her boyfriend Mark. Mark is an exchange student at Tomoe's university. He won a scholarship to study in Japan because of his high grades and excellent work as a student in London. He loves rock music, and dresses wildly, but is serious about his studies and plans to start working in his father's company after graduation.

Dear Mark,

I don't know how to write this letter. I'm afraid there's a problem with our relationship. Last week when we were in the park near my house, my mother was riding her bicycle to the store and saw us. Of course I had told her that I had made friends with an English man, but I guess she was really shocked to see me holding hands with you. She said I must be a terrible girl to be with a "guy like that, especially a foreigner". She talked about your clothes and hair.

I tried to explain, but she got very angry and said that I was trying to make excuses for my "bad boyfriend". She said that anyone with eyes could tell that you were a *furyo*.

I've been crying for two days since then, but my mother is only getting angrier. My father said that I have to trust my mother's judgment and be a good daughter. My father is usually so reasonable, but this time he simply doesn't understand.

This is terrible for me, and I can't bear to hurt you, but I'm afraid I can't see you anymore. I'm sorry, but please don't call me. Forgive me.

Love,

Tomoe

Tomoe is in a terrible position. She knows her mother is wrong about Mark, but there's no way she can communicate this to her. We can't be sure, but probably Tomoe's mother thinks she is doing the best thing for her daughter. To her, Mark is obviously bad.

Mark will probably be quite upset when he receives this letter. Not only does he lose Tomoe, but he can't communicate with her mother. Even if he could, there may be nothing he could do to change her mind. Tomoe's mother seems to have a very stereotyped view of the way Mark looks. She may have negative stereotypical ideas about foreigners too.

A **stereotype** is an oversimplified image of people from another culture. There are stereotypes not only about people from other countries, but also about skin color, age, gender, particular parts of the country, etc. Stereotypes are a natural reaction to ignorance about cultural others. If the only experience one has with Africa, for example, is seeing nature programs of wild animals and indigenous peoples living in the wilderness, then those are the images that will come to mind when thinking about Africa.

> A stereotype is an oversimplified image of people from another culture.

Stereotypes cause problems in several different ways. Because they are so simple and far away from one's experience, people we stereotype seem less human. Also, stereotypes have the tendency to become habits of perception. Once we learn to look at things in a certain way, we tend to stop taking in information that disagrees with the images we already have. Thus, even if we learn that Nairobi, Kenya is a cosmopolitan city of 1.2 million people, this may do little to change our impression of Africa as being full of lions and indigenous tribes.

Stereotypes are like weeds. They are natural, but not what we want to encourage. They get mixed in with accurate information about culture, pop up in unexpected places, and when they are small, it's hard to tell if they are stereotypes or not. Two elements that contribute to this are that stereotypes are often based on half-truths, and include judgments about cultural others based on one's own culture.

We can see this by looking at stereotypes that are sometimes heard about Japan and Japanese. Images of Japan seen by many people in other countries include employees in uniforms doing exercises together, workers packed into crowded trains, small living spaces, skyscrapers, electronic goods, and the automobile industry. Other images often associated with Japan include traditional culture like Zen Buddhism, karate and origami, as well as things like high scholastic achievement, stressful university entrance exams, and an emphasis on conformity in education and society in general.

Based on these limited images stereotypes develop. They include positive things like "Japanese are hardworking" and "Japanese are polite", as well as negative things like "Japanese are like robots", "Japanese are not creative", "Japanese are very competitive". These ideas develop about Japanese among people looking at Japan from the outside, based on the values and expectations that are normal for their culture.

For someone from a culture that emphasizes talking about oneself as a way to show friendliness, Japanese may seem unfriendly, cold, or even sneaky. For someone whose culture emphasizes individual self-expression, bowing and using honorific language may seem oppressive. For people from cultures that emphasize a connection between the present and past history, Japanese may be viewed in terms of wars and political events that happened about 50 or 100 years ago.

The stereotypes that people have of Japanese are understandable in that these images come from a lack of experience with Japan, and involve judging Japan through different cultural eyes. Still, those stereotypes are at best only partially true, and make Japanese seem less human. Since stereotypes can be unpleasant and destructive, it's important to try to understand one's own stereotypes, and then try to minimize them. There are several ways to do this.

First, learn to distinguish between a **generalization** and a **stereotype**. A generalization is a statement about a tendency of a group of people. It doesn't assume that an individual will necessarily have that quality. A stereotype is a blanket statement which doesn't leave much room for exceptions. "Japanese are workaholics" is a stereotype, while "Japanese culture places an emphasis on effort and hard work" is a generalization.

> Learn to distinguish between a generalization and a stereotype.

Be specific rather than general, and objective rather than subjective. "Foreigners are friendly" is general. "Europeans speak to strangers more often than Japanese" is more specific. "America is dangerous" is subjective (dangerous for whom? compared to where?). "There is more violent crime in the United States than in Japan" is more objective. Saying "America is dangerous" might offend an American because it is being stated as a fact, but "I feel (or "I have the impression") that America is dangerous" probably won't. It may even lead to an interesting discussion.

If you have trouble being specific and objective, then you are probably simply ignorant. Some people may say "The French are romantic" without being able to be more specific or objective. In this case, ask yourself the source of your information. Movies and vague impressions are not good sources of solid information about other cultures. What are the elements of French culture which give outsiders that impression? Body language? Values? Male-female roles? Knowing the limits of one's knowledge is the most important part of not being trapped by stereotypes.

Overcoming stereotypes is a challenge, because it means questioning ourselves. Doing so, though, enriches our lives and helps us respect others. As Tomoe learned, stereotypes can have powerful effects. If her mother had been ready to suspend judgment about Mark, she might have been able to accept him. She could have come to a deeper understanding of her daughter, even if she never particularly liked rock music, or punk fashion. Let's hope Tomoe's relationship with her mother hasn't been destroyed, even if Tomoe's relationship with Mark has been.

Did you know?

Stereotypes are closely related to racism and oppression of minority groups. They dehumanize victims and contribute to things like the apartheid policies of past governments in South Africa, the genocide against Jews and others in Germany during World War II, the internment of Japanese Americans in the United States, and the massacre of Koreans in the aftermath of the Great Kanto Earthquake.

Focus on Content

1. Based on what the text says, the real source of the problems between Tomoe and her mother come from:
   a. Mark's appearance.
   b. Mark being a foreigner.
   c. Tomoe's mother's preconceived ideas.
   d. Tomoe's mothers cruel attitude.

2. According to the text, stereotypes come from:
   a. limited experience with cultural others.
   b. a conservative personality.
   c. a fear of foreigners.
   d. Japanese traditional values.

3. "Stereotypes become habits of perception" in lines 3-4, page 17 means:
   a. we only see positive things about a culture.
   b. we learn our point of view from our culture.
   c. we modify our opinions when we have more experiences.
   d. our view of something doesn't change despite additional information.

4. A possible example of the text's statement in lines 16-17, page 17 that "stereotypes include judgments about cultural others based on one's own culture" might be:
   a. saying that in India many languages are spoken.
   b. feeling that Canada is beautiful because a Canadian said so.
   c. feeling that Koreans are strange because dogs are sometimes eaten in Korea.
   d. feeling (as a Japanese) that Japanese culture is best.

5. One difference between a generalization and a stereotype is that:
   a. stereotypes are wrong.
   b. generalizations allow for exceptions.
   c. stereotypes are specific.
   d. generalizations depend more on a person's point of view.

Culture Quiz

Evaluate these statements. Are they stereotypes or generalizations?

1. Italians are passionate.
2. Chinese culture values saving face.
3. Japanese are shy.
4. Family relationships are important in Korean culture.
5. The Middle-East is violent.
6. Old people are conservative.
7. Women talk a lot.
8. Being reserved is important in parts of British culture.

Activities

Take these general and/or subjective statements and **make** them more specific and/or objective. Then **compare** your answers with a partner.

Example: *In Japan everybody eats rice.*
      becomes
      In Japan many people eat rice nearly every day.
      or,
      Rice is an important and common food in Japan.

1. Japan is small.
2. Australians are friendly.
3. People from Kansai are loud.
4. Japan is rich.
5. Small towns are boring.
6. Women are polite.
7. Everybody has a gun in the United States.
8. Japan is safe.
9. Japanese love American movies and music.
10. Japanese are conformist.
11. Russians love Vodka.

Negative stereotypes:

These are some stereotypical statements. Many or all of them are offensive. Look at each statement. Do you think some people you know might consciously or unconsciously agree? Make a list of negative stereotypes that you have heard. Discuss where they come from.

    Western women are too strong.
    People from rural areas are simple-minded.
    Chinese are all the same.
    Westerners are more attractive than Asians.
    Americans are loud.
    Young people are irresponsible.

Chapter 4
Words, Words, Words

"Yes, the words themselves are easy, but not the subtle cultural differences."

Learning Not to be "Otonashii"

Yuki is a young Japanese woman studying English at a small university in Colorado in the U.S. She was interviewed by a school newspaper after being chosen by her teachers as "outstanding student" because of the remarkably rapid improvement in her English. In this excerpt, she was asked about vocabulary and learning to think in English.

Hard words are easier. For lectures or reading textbooks I need to learn complicated abstract words. It takes time to look them up and remember them, but they are very straightforward. Words like "industrialize" or "socialization" are impersonal and so it's easy to translate and use them. Unfortunately, they don't carry much feeling and don't help me make friends or get along well with people.

I have a language exchange with a girl—maybe I should say woman—who is studying Japanese. We discussed a word in Japanese, *otonashii*, for an hour. Her book said it means gentle or meek and is used as a compliment, especially for women. I told her I think I am *otonashii*, but she told me that I'm not meek at all. She said being meek meant acting like a frightened mouse.

I try to get the cultural feeling when I speak English, and not depend on Japanese ideas and feelings translated into English. I like the word "caring" in English to describe myself, even if it doesn't match the word *otonashii*. I think I am a very flexible person—oh, I wonder if that sounds too boastful—and I try to catch the feeling of words. I test them to check how they fit me, and wear them around for a while like some new shoes. After a while they become comfortable enough to become a part of me.

As Yuki has discovered, the meaning of words depends on culture. People who don't speak a foreign language well may think of a foreign language in functional terms—a way to convey objective information using a different set of sounds. In fact, it's much more interesting than that. When we learn to speak another language, we have to also learn how to change our way of looking at the world, and our way of thinking and interacting. It is like putting on a new pair of glasses which helps us see everything in a new and different way.

Words are rich in cultural meaning. Many have no foreign language equivalent because they are so tied to a particular culture. To have a clear understanding of *furoshiki*, one has to know how a *furoshiki* is used and its origin. Words related to values are also strongly connected to culture. In the U.S., "freedom" is associated with being an individual and making choices to find personal fulfillment. In France, *liberte* is an important political ideal with historical meaning going back to the 18th century. In Japan, *jiyu* has a flavor given to it by Japanese values.

On the surface the simple word "teacher", for example, may seem the same as *sensei*, but it isn't at all. In English it's usually rude to address someone simply as "teacher", while in Japanese the opposite can be true. *Sensei* implies a mastery, and literally means "life senior". "Teacher" is more simply a job description, and not a title.

> English speakers expect different things from their **teachers** than Japanese students do from their **sensei**.

"Teachers" may expect more independence from their students, and less deference than a *sensei*. The influence of Confucian ideas can be found in *sensei*, while individualism and a valuing of egalitarianism can be found in "teacher". Even simple words can be a reflection in miniature of a whole culture, and a great place to start cultural exploration.

LANGUAGE AND COMMUNICATION

It can seem that when speaking, words and sentences are a way of passing information from one person to another, like tossing a ball. In fact, nothing really travels except the sound waves, which form a code requiring extensive background knowledge to fully understand. A more accurate way to describe words and communication is to say that words create meaning that is already inside the listener. Of course original ideas and new information can be passed between speakers, but only within the limits of the shared symbolic framework of the language.

When Yuki's friend who is studying Japanese hears the word *otonashii*, she associates it with two English words: "meek" and "gentle". The meaning of *otonashii* has been only partially communicated because Yuki's friend doesn't have the cultural background for deep understanding. Using *otonashii* well requires getting a feeling for it within Japanese culture. Every language has words like this, and learning to use them well can be an exciting cultural adventure.

> Language often becomes a symbolic battleground.

Language can also become a symbolic battleground for social issues because its use reflects our values. The word *kanai* literally means "in the house" and has been criticized as unfair to women. In English, the word Ms. became common in the 1970s as a way to refer to a woman without indicating her marital status (as Miss and Mrs. do). The history of civil rights for the descendants of slaves brought from Africa can be traced through time by the words considered appropriate at different times in history: nigger, negro, Negro, Black and currently African American, or, as a broader category, persons of color.

Language not only reflects values, but also identifies someone as a member of particular cultural groups. Many people from Osaka are proud of their Kansai Japanese, and the language of the residents of Kyushu, Okinawa or Aomori is connected to their identity, lifestyles and values. When a cultural group loses its language, as has happened with the Ainu, and is happening in Okinawa, a precious source of creativity and identity is lost forever.

For someone like Yuki studying English, it's important to see how learning a language also means learning a culture. There's always a danger of misunderstanding caused by not appreciating the cultural associations of words. More importantly though, a new language is like a door into another cultural world, in which we can express ourselves in new ways and discover a self we didn't know existed before. This is what Yuki is doing. Whether we say she is *otanashii* or "caring", she is using language not as a barrier, but as a vehicle for her cultural exploration.

Did you know? 1-13

The word "**rap**" was a slang word meaning "talk" which came out of African American culture in the U.S. While it still has that meaning, it now more commonly refers to a style of music in which lyrics are spoken rather than sung.

"**Blue**", meaning to feel down, also comes from U.S. African American culture, from the musical tradition of the Blues, which has its roots in Africa, and was played as far back as the 19th century by wandering black musicians.

"**Gay**" traditionally meant happy or joyous, and is still used in that way. Now, however, it more commonly refers to homosexuality, and is not generally considered derogatory.

"**Cool**", meaning stylish or good, is considered slang, but first became popular more than 60 years ago among (primarily African American) jazz musicians.

Focus on Content

1. Why does Yuki say in line 6, page 23 that "hard words are easier"?
    a. She likes difficult subjects like economics.
    b. Because she has strong feelings about "hard" words.
    c. Because "hard" words are less personal and so easier to translate and use.
    d. Because "easy" words are very straightforward.

2. According to the text, which of the following words is most likely to be difficult to translate directly?
    a. economics
    b. automobile
    c. book
    d. independence

3. According to the text, speaking is *not* like tossing a ball to someone because:
    a. the message is contained within the words themselves.
    b. meaning is contained within the sound waves.
    c. meaning is constructed inside the listener.
    d. it's impossible to get a totally accurate image of meaning using words.

4. According to the text, people argue about language because:
    a. language use represents the attitudes of the people using it.
    b. in the U.S. values are changing.
    c. the meaning of words doesn't change.
    d. there are racial problems in the U.S.

5. Many words cannot be translated easily into another language because:
    a. every culture is different.
    b. understanding them requires cultural background knowledge.
    c. words reflect the culture they come from.
    d. all of the above

Culture Quiz

Test your intuition about the subtle meaning of simple words in English.

1. The word *pioneer* often creates the impression in a native English speaker's mind of:
   a. a woman.
   b. a man.
   c. either a woman or a man.
   d. a man, woman or animal.

2. Typically, the form of address Miss is seen as being:
   a. more conservative than Ms.
   b. more progressive than Ms.
   c. always value neutral.
   d. always offensive.

3. Currently, the term African American is seen as being more appropriate than Negro because:
   a. Negro sounds like nigger.
   b. Negro is an older word.
   c. Negro is racial, while African American emphasizes ethnicity (culture and history).
   d. The term African American was popular as Africa was more reported on in the media.

4. There are many kinds of birds, but which of the following types is the most "birdlike" for English speakers (i.e., which image does the word "bird" bring to mind)?
   a. pigeon
   b. sparrow
   c. penguin
   d. eagle

Activities

1. **Look** at the following one-word Japanese translation for each of the following five English words. What difference in nuance, or in how these words might be used, can you find between the English words and the Japanese?

obstacle	jama
to hold back	enryo (suru)
harmony	wa
endurance	gaman
in-group	nakama

2. **Choose five words** in Japanese that you think are very important to understanding Japanese culture. Write a definition to explain these five words to someone from another country. Include how the words are used, and why you think they are important.

Chapter 5
Communication Without Words

Young people and graffiti—Tokyo, Japan

Trusting Your Eyes   1-14

   This photograph was taken by an American visiting Japan, when he was walking under a bridge near the Tama River in Tokyo. One of the young people seen waved, and the American turned and snapped a picture for fun, without paying much attention. After developing the photo, he commented to a Japanese friend that it seemed a sad picture. His friend couldn't understand what he meant. Eventually, after discussing what gave each of them different impressions about the photo, they decided that maybe cultural difference had caused them to get different meanings from the same photo. Look at the photo again to see if you can find two possible interpretations.

   The American thought the photo was sad because he felt that the two people on the right looked very unhappy, and that they were being ignored by their friends. The Japanese friend of the photographer was convinced that the two young people on the right were not unhappy, they were simply cover-

ing their faces because they were shy or uncomfortable being photographed. He argued that in Japan young people often go out in groups, and that having a photo taken as a group is very common, but that not everyone wants to have their photo taken every time. He said that he himself had felt that way when
out with his friends. Eventually, the American conceded that his Japanese friend probably was better able to judge, but still found it somehow difficult to change the way he looked at the picture. It still seemed sad, even though he knew it probably was a misinterpretation.

1-15 Because we cannot ask the young people in the photo why they were sitting as they were, we can't be sure of whether the American or his Japanese friend (or neither) was right. This shows us how two people from different cultures can see the same thing and interpret it in very different ways. This kind of misunderstanding is one of the dangers with nonverbal communication.

Nonverbal communication happens without words, is influenced by culture, and is so often taken for granted that it takes having someone disagree with you in order to discover the process. It involves the meaning we give to the things that we see. Two important elements of nonverbal communication are gestures and body language.

Gestures are used intentionally to communicate a specific meaning, and are usually associated with a particular word or expression. Many books on intercultural communication focus on comparing gestures in different countries. For example, in Japan people refer to themselves by pointing to their nose, while in English-speaking countries people point at their chest. Japanese cross their forearms to indicate *dame* or *batsu* while this gesture has no mean-

---

Nonverbal communication:
Communication (intentional and unintentional) without the use of sound. For example: through body language, gestures, etc.

ing in English. These differences are interesting, and it's good to know them, but they seldom cause serious communication problems.

> Our faces, body movements, use of space all reflect how we feel.

Body language, on the other hand, is unconscious and is used to communicate not ideas, but our inner mental and emotional state. Our faces, body movements and use of space all reflect how we feel. Many people can easily tell if a friend is not feeling happy simply by looking at him or her. When people do this, they are reading the other person and the environment, but usually without knowing exactly what gives the impression that the friend is not happy. It could be a subtle facial expression, body posture, being somewhere unusual for that person (sitting alone on the ground, for example), the lack of normal behavior (like offering a greeting). All of these things are felt intuitively, and they don't depend on language.

No matter what you do (or don't do), and no matter where you are, people who notice you read you and receive some impression about you. That impression may be wrong, but the process of getting meaning from feeling our environment never stops. A spy who dresses like a tourist in order not to be noticed while taking pictures is taking advantage of this.

We can read the feelings and intentions of friends and family fairly well, and strangers from our own culture to some degree, but people from other cultures can be difficult or impossible to read accurately. The reason comes down to more than differences in individual personality. Different cultures use different body language. A

> People from other cultures can be difficult or impossible to read accurately.

smile may mean embarrassment in Japan, yet be misunderstood as friendliness by an American. Keeping one's face expressionless when uncertain may work in Japan but seem cold or angry in another culture.

Behavior that is obviously different from our own may cause miscommunication, but at least we notice it and can think about its meaning. A Japanese who visits Saudi Arabia might notice men holding hands. By asking, he or she will learn that it is usual for male friends to hold hands, and that it has nothing to do with homosexuality, as it might in some other countries. At least this Japanese visitor realizes that there was probably a culture difference involved. Less obvious difference can cause serious trouble because its cultural roots aren't noticed.

One subtle yet powerful element of nonverbal communication is the use of space. An English (or Japanese) visitor to the Middle East may feel people are friendly, or pushy, or even aggressive, in part because (same sex) touching is more common in Arab culture than in British (or Japanese). The same is true in China, and may give Japanese visitors unconsciously negative impressions of the Chinese. The distance two acquaintances stand apart when talking in Spain or Israel is less than in Japan, and can give the impression of pushiness. For people from those countries, on the other hand, Japanese may seem stiff, cold or unfriendly.

> Body Language: Posture, touching, facial expressions, etc. interpreted by others.

Eye contact also communicates a lot, often without being noticed. Eye contact is considered a sign of respect in much of English-speaking culture. A child being scolded by a parent in the U.S. might be told "Look at me when I'm talking to you!" On the other hand, a Japanese child who looks his or her parent in the eye while being scolded might be considered insolent.

The biggest challenge when dealing with differences in nonverbal behavior is the need to combine the ability to be perceptive with the ability to be detached. Without being detached, we may jump to inaccurate conclusions—e.g. "Wow, Arabs are pushy", or "Wow, Japanese are shy"—without stopping to consider if the reason that one is reacting that way is a lack of understanding of how Arabs or Japanese communicate among themselves. As we learn the communication patterns of others, we can use our bodies to join in the intricate dance of communication.

Did you know?

The facial expressions which express very basic emotions—anger, fear, joy, etc.—are identified accurately by people from all cultures. Basic facial expressions are universal in interpretation, but more subtle facial expressions are not. Also, different cultures have different expectations about when and how to show certain emotions. Japanese and Americans both recognize that a smile means happiness, but while in Japan a smile is often used to show (or cover) embarrassment, in the U.S. it's used that way much less. In some cultures, a man may be expected to smile only very seldom. This doesn't mean that he never feels happy; he simply learns not to smile in certain situations. In general, human universals don't cause miscommunication, but variation often does.

Focus on Content

1. According to the ideas presented in the text, the photograph communicated something different to the American and the Japanese because:
    a. the American was not a careful observer.
    b. there was no way to ask the people in the photo.
    c. nonverbal communication is often taken for granted.
    d. their interpretation was influenced by differences in their background.

2. According to the text, gestures:
    a. are the same everywhere.
    b. cause many obvious problems in intercultural communication.
    c. are relatively obvious, so cause few problems in intercultural communication.
    d. create subtle problems in intercultural communication.

3. According to the text, if we are watched we communicate because:
    a. people can read someone with a similar background.
    b. people's behavior depends on personality.
    c. our presence and our behavior are interpreted by others.
    d. we sometimes decide to get meaning from our environment.

4. According to the text, body language:
    a. is easy to notice and analyze.
    b. sometimes communicates things we don't mean to.
    c. is the simplest and easiest way to communicate.
    d. is the same all over the world.

5. We may jump to inaccurate conclusions if we:
    a. aren't confident of our ability to interpret other's actions.
    b. react to something and then carefully analyze our feelings.
    c. don't think about the cultural causes of our interpretations.
    d. don't use our bodies when communicating.

5 : Communication Without Words

Culture Quiz

Test your intuition about some elements of nonverbal communication in other countries.

1. In much of U.S. culture, the usual distance between acquaintances standing and talking is about:
    a. 75 centimeters.
    b. 95 centimeters.
    c. 115 centimeters.
    d. 135 centimeters.

2. When using a hand gesture to indicate height in Mexico, the following hand positions are used. Match them with what they are used for.

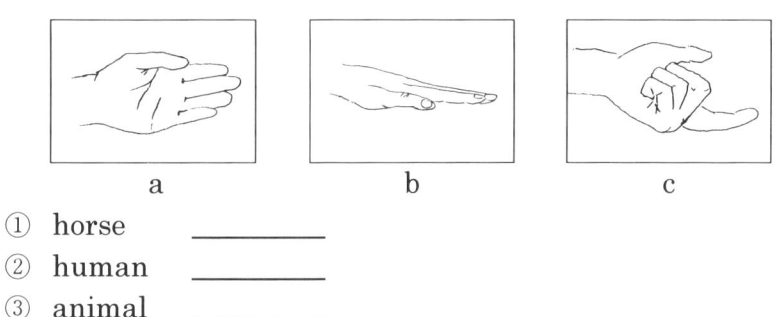

    a   b   c

    ① horse   _____
    ② human   _____
    ③ animal   _____

3. In England, same-sex touching in public is
    a. more common than in Spain.
    b. less common than in Spain.
    c. less common between women than in Spain.
    d. less common between men but not women than in Spain.

4. English speakers report that Japanese use of eye contact sometimes gives the impression of:
    a. weakness.
    b. dishonesty.
    c. nervousness.
    d. all of the above.

Activities

1. **Make** a list of as many gestures that you use as you can.

2. **Act out a conversation** at a party for three minutes. Converse normally, except stand 10~20 centimeters closer than you normally would. Discuss how it feels and what you would do if speaking with a foreigner who usually speaks at this distance.

3. **Act out a job interview**. The interviewer should ask many questions of the interviewee, but never look at him or her in the face. Switch roles and then discuss the impression the boss gives. Compare this to how it might feel for someone from a culture with a lot of eye contact who speaks to someone with less.

Chapter 6
Diversity

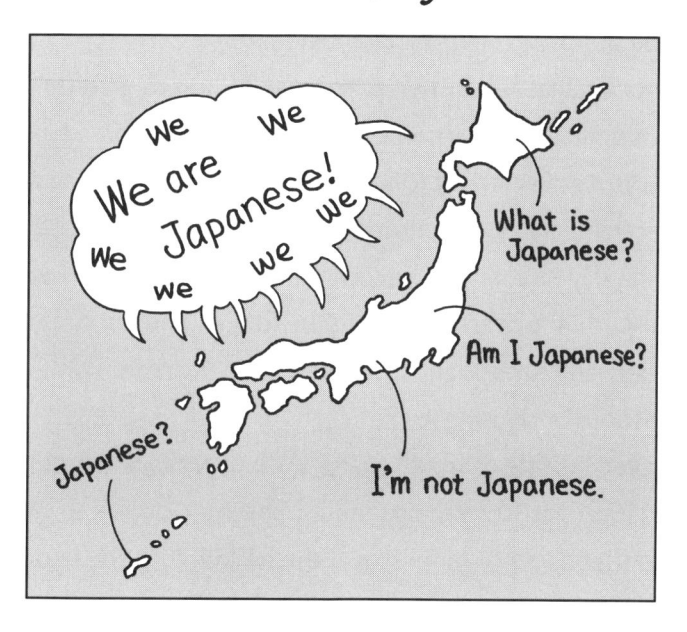

Kiyomi and Sanmi's Story　　1-17

 The other stories in this book are fiction, written to illustrate a certain point about intercultural communication. The following, however, is based on the experience of a real person. Only the names have been changed.

 Kiyomi grew up like many other girls in Japan. She had her favorite foods, her favorite friends and her favorite subjects in school. She also had her dream for the future: she wanted to be a diplomat. As a child, though, she couldn't have understood the frustrations and fear she would face because of a secret—something that her parents knew but hadn't told her. It would change her life forever.

 One day in junior high school a friend approached her and said, "I heard you are Korean. Is that true?" Kiyomi was confused. When she went home that day she asked her parents and they told her that, yes, she was in fact Korean.

From then on Kiyomi began to live in fear. She was afraid of being left out, and so she hid her background. She knew little about the circumstances under which many thousands of Koreans came to Japan during the time of her grandparents. She wasn't interested in history, war or politics, but she couldn't escape them.

Another shock came when her parents told her to give up her dream of becoming a diplomat. She learned that because she wasn't a Japanese citizen, she couldn't hold a government job, including being a diplomat working in the Ministry of Foreign Affairs. It seemed incredible to her, and she continued to believe that one day she would become a diplomat. Kiyomi was bright and entered a well-known private university in Tokyo. She continued to hide her Korean identity, and although she knew her Korean name—Sanmi—she wouldn't have thought of using it.

Then, however, her life changed again. At university she met members of a student association for Korean students. She met others in her own situation and found friends who understood the hidden fear she had lived with for so many years. For the first time, she began to feel pride in her identity.

She came to the decision to tell her other friends about her identity. As she gained confidence she became more comfortable. Being Korean, and the understanding she found from her Korean friends, became more important to her. She even decided to use her Korean name, in spite of the trouble it caused her. Once, applying for a part-time job using her Korean name, she was rejected. A few weeks later she applied at the same place using her Japanese name, and was accepted.

Kiyomi/Sanmi is now in her twenties, and gives speeches at schools so teachers and students can have a better understanding of the difficulties faced by Koreans born in Japan. She no longer hides her name and background. Kiyomi/Sanmi doesn't speak Korean, and her personality, values and interests are the same as many Japanese women her age. Perhaps for that reason, the question of her Korean identity has been especially difficult for her. She never felt different, but was made to feel different, and had to discover a deeper sense of self—one that didn't depend on choosing between saying "I am Japanese" and "I am Korean".

It is still impossible (with a few exceptions) for Kiyomi/Sanmi to be a diplomat or employee for the national government. The political, social and historical questions involving Koreans in Japan are far beyond the scope of this book, but the issue of cultural identity, and being different, are directly related to intercultural communication, and are the subject of this chapter.

This chapter is about diversity. Diversity simply means difference within a group that shares an identity. Japanese culture emphasizes similarity within groups. In spite of social change, being a member of a certain group is still very important, whether one is a high school student or company employee. This allows for cooperation, encourages closeness and good relations between like-minded people. Some credit this cultural emphasis for Japan's phenomenal economic success since WWII.

> Japanese culture emphasizes similarity within groups.

This tendency, though, can create an atmosphere of exclusion. It's important to consider what role this plays in social issues such as bullying, returnees, Koreans born in Japan, support for the disabled, preservation of Ainu culture, and so on. Sometimes, as with bullying, a simple lack of acceptance creates discrimination. Other times, as with returnees, there are questions of how to adapt institutions, such as schools, to deal with the needs and abilities of the different member.

In Japan, diversity and discrimination are often associated with obvious racial and social issues like apartheid in South Africa, or race relations in the United States. When we study intercultural communication, however, we see that all cultures distinguish between one's own group (in-groups) and outsiders (out-groups), and that this natural human tendency also creates negative effects,

DIFFERENT REALITIES

such as stereotypes and prejudice.

The line between feeling someone is different and discrimination is difficult to draw clearly. Feeling sorry for someone with a disability may seem natural, or even kind. People with disabilities, however, often say that pity is a form of discrimination because it focuses too much attention on one part of that person—their blindness, for example—and it ignores all of their other human qualities. This over-emphasis on difference prevents us from forming close relationships and enriching our lives with the other person's experiences and abilities.

> The line between feeling someone is different and discrimination is difficult to draw clearly.

To form relationships with people who are different from oneself requires two elements: recognition of commonality, and recognition of difference. Relating to others requires that we have something in common so we can share our lives and experiences. With nothing in common communication is impossible. At the same time, recognizing and respecting difference encourages the acceptance necessary for meaningful relationships.

Ultimately, good intercultural communication means discovering points in common and points of difference, and using both as the basis for our relationships. If I am a Japanese university student getting to know a Chinese university student, what experiences and human qualities do we share that can bring us closer? What differences can I discover to help me understand my new friend (and myself) better?

Forming this kind of relationship is demanding. It requires reflection: Who am I? What are my values? What is my style of communication? What does it mean to be Japanese

> Good intercultural communication means discovering points in common and points of difference.

(Korean, Swedish, etc.)? This is not a question of being nice or good, it's a responsibility towards others—whether someone like Kiyomi whose difference is invisible, or someone in a wheelchair who needs a door opened. Recognizing diversity allows us to fully share our humanity.

Did You Know? 1-19

The population of India is 920 million, more than seven times that of Japan. There are 16 official languages, including Hindi, English, Bengali, Punjabi and Sanskrit. There are 24 languages which have more than 1 million speakers, and more than 300 languages overall. The population is made up of Hindus (82%), Muslims (12%), Sikhs (2%), Jains (less than 1%), and Christians (3%). Although Buddhism started in India, less than 1% of the population is Buddhist. In addition to linguistic and religious diversity, there is rural/urban diversity as well as tremendous socio-economic diversity. India is a secular democratic state with free elections having determined leadership since Mahatma Ghandi led it to independence from Great Britain in 1947. Social harmony has been weakened by violent clashes, in particular between Hindus and Muslims.

(Taken from *Culturgrams*, 1995, David M. Kennedy Center for International Studies, Brigham Young University)

Focus on Content

1. According to the text, Japan's emphasis on similarity within groups:
   a. needs to be changed.
   b. is only found in Japan.
   c. prevents Japanese economic success.
   d. can be both constructive and destructive.

2. According to the text, studying intercultural communication shows us that discrimination:
   a. exists primarily in countries like South Africa and the U.S.
   b. is a consequence of natural human tendencies.
   c. is related strictly to race.
   d. does not exist in Japan.

3. According to the text, deciding whether something is discrimination requires:
   a. being kind.
   b. emphasizing difference.
   c. considering the issue from the other person's point of view.
   d. denying difference.

4. According to the text, good intercultural communication requires:
   a. focusing primarily on universal human qualities.
   b. emphasizing ways the other is different from oneself.
   c. looking for neither difference nor similarity.
   d. looking for both difference and similarity.

5. According to the ideas in this chapter, self understanding is important in intercultural communication because:
   a. Japanese have a unique communication style.
   b. it helps us identify similarity and difference.
   c. it makes us easier to get along with.
   d. it helps us express our culture's ideas.

6 : Diversity

Culture Quiz

Test your knowledge of diversity around the world.

1. How many native speakers of the Ainu language are there?
   a. 0
   b. 2
   c. 20
   d. 200

2. How many countries belong to the United Nations?
   a. 45
   b. 115
   c. 185
   d. 255

3. Around what percentage of the population of Hawaii is of Japanese ancestry?
   a. 1/20th
   b. 1/10th
   c. 1/5th
   d. 1/3rd

4. According to data provided by religious organizations, how many Christians are there in Japan?
   a. about 50,000
   b. about 500,000
   c. about 1,500,000
   d. about 15,000,000

5. About how many Chinese do not speak Mandarin?
   a. more than 300,000
   b. more than 3,000,000
   c. more than 30,000,000
   d. more than 300,000,000

Activities

1. **Think** of several people whom you know personally that are as different from each other as possible—for example, a traditionally-minded old uncle and a high school friend who loves popular fashions. What kinds of disagreements might they have because of their differences? **Act out** a conversation between the two.

2. **Make** a list of as many cultural groups within Japan as you can.

3. **What problems** with things like finding work, finding housing, making friends might the following people have when coming to live in Japan?

   ★An American coming to work as an assistant English teacher in a rural high school.

   ★A Brazilian of Japanese ancestry coming to work in a factory.

   ★A Chinese college student coming to study at a university.

Chapter 7
Perception

Panel 1: "I must be a pessimist. My glass looks half empty." / "No, wrong again."

Panel 2: "You mean you think I'm actually an optimist?"

Panel 3: "No, it actually **is** half empty." / "......"

Touching

John is an American from San Francisco living in Tokyo. He's talking with his girlfriend Mariko while they watch a TV drama. In one scene, a young woman is sitting in her room sobbing bitterly about breaking up with her boyfriend. Her best friend is sitting close to her, looking on with a sad and sympathetic expression on her face.

John: This scene really shows how affection-starved Japanese culture is. Her friend doesn't even put her arm around that girl, or hug her or anything. She just sits there and watches.

Mariko: Well, she's keeping her company. She's her best friend.

John: That's what I mean. Even though she's her best friend, she's not affectionate. I hardly ever see affection in Japan.

Mariko: Hmm. Well, I guess affection is private, so you don't see it.

John: Yeah, maybe, but did your parents hug you as a child, or show physical affection to each other? I mean, I've never felt my family is warm or affectionate, but at least I got hugs from my parents.

Mariko: Well, my family doesn't hug much. I've never seen my parents kiss. I suppose they are pretty average in that way. But my family is very warm and affectionate. It's just shown differently.

John: But don't you think that touching is a universal way of showing closeness to someone?

Mariko: I guess so.

John: And don't you think it's true that Japanese touch each other less than, say, Americans?

Mariko: Well, yes, I suppose so. I don't see Japanese touching as much as Americans, like in public, or even among family members.

John: That's what I mean. It's just not an affectionate culture.

Mariko: Well, I'm not sure. (Pause) Do you mean you want me to be more affectionate?

John: Huh?

2-2 Mariko doesn't seem totally convinced by John's analysis of Japanese culture. It may be that she doesn't quite feel comfortable with John's direct, logical style of argument. Maybe she doesn't feel confident giving opinions about American culture, especially because John's mind may already be made up. John, on the other hand, may prefer that Mariko give stronger opinions, and may even find Mariko's last question completely off the point.

One thing is certain, however. Their conversation reflects the difficulty of understanding our own **perception**. In intercultural situations, the meaning of some thing or action may seem obvious, yet be perceived by others in a different way. For John, his observation that Japanese generally touch each other less than Americans obviously indicates that Japanese are not affectionate. While Mariko seems to agree with the observation that Japanese are less physical, she seems to be unconvinced of his conclusion.

> The meaning of an action may seem obvious, yet be perceived by others in a different way.

The difference between our experience, i.e. the information we get through our senses, and the interpretation of that information, is very important. Our experience can be described objectively, but the interpretation of that experience is subjective. The difference between **describing** and **interpreting** is the difference between saying "He is frowning" and "He is unhappy".

When we are with someone from a similar cultural background to our own, we share a framework, or standard, for interpreting our experience. In this case, distinguishing between description and interpretation may be unimportant. If John were speaking to another American, he might get immediate agreement. Because for John, and probably many Americans, physical contact is an important way to show affection between adults, he is unconsciously using this as a standard for his conclusions about Japanese culture.

> The difference between describing and interpreting is the difference between saying "He is frowning" and "He is unhappy".

Mariko said her family is warm, even though they are not physical. It seems that for Mariko, the amount of touching is a less important measure of affection than for John. These unrecognized differences in standards of interpretation are causing difficulty in their communication.

Perception is a learned process. Colors are the same everywhere, but different cultures divide the spectrum up in different ways. In some languages, blue and black are seen as two shades of the same

DIFFERENT REALITIES

color. This may seem strange, but if you look at a clear sky at dusk you can see this blue/black color.

In Japan children draw pictures of the sun and color it red, while children in some other countries color their suns yellow. These differences exist because we learn categories of perception from our culture. Our physical environment is objective, but not always perceived in the same way. Perception is also a habitual process. Once we get used to looking at things in a certain way, it's often difficult to change. We occasionally make perceptual "mistakes", like seeing a bird flutter in a bush, only to realize that in fact it's a piece of paper caught in a branch. Once we see it as paper, it's nearly impossible to go back to seeing it as a bird.

> What color is the sun?

If the interpretation of our experience is cultural at the simple level of colors, then how much more so for interpreting people's actions. Our culture teaches us a system which tells us the meaning of different actions in different circumstances. For John, a lack of touching means that Japanese are not affectionate.

This particular case is made more confusing because in Japan, touching *is* sometimes used to show affections, so Americans may appear in some absolute way to be more affectionate than Japanese. However, as John even admits, the hugs he got as a child didn't make him feel his family was affectionate. Mariko, on the other hand, didn't get hugs, but feels her family is warm and affectionate. The best way to understand the behavior of someone from a different culture is to understand how people in that other culture might interpret that behavior.

> The best way to understand the behavior of someone from a different culture is to understand how the people in that other culture might interpret that behavior.

Touching is clearly used in different ways in Japan and the U.S., and this is the source of John and Mariko's difficulties in agreeing on their interpretations of what they observed. Let's hope that Mariko's last question was unnecessary, and that this is as far as their problems go.

Did you know?

Time—In most English-speaking cultures, as well as Japanese culture, time is perceived as something concrete and objective, which exists independent of humans, and can therefore properly be used to control behavior ("Let's try to finish by five!"). Therefore, to break off a conversation with someone in order to keep an appointment at a certain time is generally not considered rude. However, in some other cultures, like Latin cultures, time is considered to be an artificial, and therefore, subservient concept when compared with human interaction. For this reason, in Latin culture, it can easily be considered rude to break off a conversation using a statement about time as a reason. Because of different concepts of time, Latins are sometimes considered irresponsible or lazy by, for example, Americans or Japanese. On the other hand, Latins may see Americans or Japanese as inhuman and machinelike.

Focus on Content

1. The story about John and Mariko reflects the difficulty of understanding our own perception because:
   a. they both agreed on what they saw, but not on what it meant.
   b. John and Mariko aren't trying to understand each other.
   c. John has stronger opinions than Mariko.
   d. Mariko's experience with Americans is limited.

2. The difference between describing and interpreting is like:
   a. the difference between Japanese and American perceptions.
   b. the difference between Mariko's opinion and John's opinion.
   c. the difference between "he hit him" and "he is angry".
   d. the difference between "they are happy" and "they are sad".

3. The fact that in Japan children draw suns as red and in some other countries as yellow shows us that:
   a. the appearance of the sun depends on the country.
   b. the way we perceive our environment is influenced by culture.
   c. the school systems of Japan and other countries are different.
   d. our physical environment is subjective.

4. According to the text, John's conclusion that Japanese are not affectionate is caused by:
   a. problems in his relationship with Mariko.
   b. the fact that Japanese are not affectionate.
   c. John's lack of affection as a child.
   d. interpreting his experience with Japanese based on American standards.

5. John didn't feel that his family was affectionate, yet seems to feel that:
   a. his family is a special case.
   b. his family showed affection in other ways.
   c. his family was still more affectionate than Japanese families.
   d. his family simply didn't show their feelings.

Culture Quiz

Test your intuition about perception.

1. In English, the color green is usually associated with which emotion?
    a. anger
    b. envy
    c. happiness
    d. sadness

2. In Taiwan, blinking while someone is talking is sometimes considered:
    a. unusual
    b. funny
    c. interesting
    d. impolite

3. Which of the following Japanese concepts (perceptual categories) does not exist in English?
    a. *amae* (as a type of relationship)
    b. *shibui* (as a quality to describe a person)
    c. *wabi* (as an aesthetic quality)
    d. all of the above

4. In Thailand, it is rude to pat a child on the head because:
    a. it is seen as a sign of anger.
    b. the hand is considered the dirtiest part of the body.
    c. the head is considered the most sacred part of the body.
    d. it symbolizes stupidity.

5. In an American university, a student who asks the professor for permission to leave the class and go to the restroom may often be perceived as:
    a. highly respectful.
    b. shameful.
    c. childish.
    d. normal.

DIFFERENT REALITIES

Activities

1. **Who is this?**
   Look at this picture. What do you see? Is it the same as what other students see?

2. **Three or two?**
   Look at this drawing for several seconds. Then cover it and draw it from memory. Why is it difficult?

   Drawing from *Your Amazing Senses*,
   Ron and Atie Van der Meer, Macmillan, 1987

3. **Perception and Images**

   Step one   There are two photographs on the next page. Look at them briefly, then cover them up. Which of these two men would you rather become friends with? Discuss what gives you a positive or negative impression of each of these two men.

   Step two   Make a list of what you see in the two pictures. For example, "In picture A I see a man who is . . .". After making your list, compare it with the list below each of the pictures. You may disagree with some items. Add anything you want to your list.

   Step three   Divide the statements on your list into the categories of "description" or "interpretation". For example: *A man is sitting down* (description); *A drunk man is asleep* (interpretation).

Step four Show your list to others and discuss the things you disagree on. What dangers are there in confusing description and interpretation? Have you ever been misunderstood based on someone else's interpretation of you?

A

A man is sitting down.
He is drunk.
He is holding a cellular phone.
He is asleep.
He is wearing a cap.
He is a college student.
He is leaning against the trash can.
He is sick.
He is a wild young person.
He is wearing a plaid shirt.
His hair is long.
His hair is sticking out from under his cap.
He is dirty.

B

A man is standing up.
He is holding a newspaper.
He is handsome.
He is looking for something.
He is bored.
He has short hair.
He thinks that he is cool.
He is waiting for something.
He is standing in the sun.
He is a normal person.
He is leaning against something.
He is sad.
He is serious.

Chapter 8
Communication Styles (1)

After years of feeling ignored at breakfast,
Martha finally resorts to sign language.

Love on the Rocks

2-4

    Steve is a 24-year-old assistant English teacher in a high school in Saitama. His girlfriend, Kumiko, is a 4th year university student. Steve's friend Shinji has been dating Koh, Kumiko's best friend. Unfortunately, Shinji and Koh have been having relationship trouble. Steve and Kumiko are discussing their friends' problems.

Steve: Did you hear about the latest?

Kumiko: You mean their dinner on Friday?

Steve: Yeah. Shinji said he spent three hours listening to Koh complain. He said Koh is trying to force him to end their relationship.

Kumiko: Really? I don't think so. Koh came over to my place after that. She was really upset, crying and everything. We stayed up until three talking. She said she was trying to explain to him how she felt, so

	they could improve their relationship.
Steve:	Hmm, well Shinji came over too. He was drunk—said he went to a bar after Koh went home. I was afraid he was going to throw up on my new sofa.
Kumiko:	Gross. (Pause) Koh thinks he doesn't care about her. He never talks to her even though he's really outgoing when he's with his guy friends.
Steve:	Well, that's 'cause they are guys. He can't talk about guy stuff with her. She's always being nosy. She came over and cleaned his apartment when he wasn't even home.
Kumiko:	Well, if he doesn't want her to do something then he should say so. She was trying to show affection. He should have some appreciation.
Steve:	I think he's trying to be a good boyfriend by not saying anything. He figures you just have to put up with girls' soft attitude.
Kumiko:	I think he's just trying to act cool. He could be more open.
Steve:	Well, Koh could certainly be a little less talkative. She's kind of . . .
Kumiko:	Steve . . .
Steve:	Yeah?
Kumiko:	Let's not start.
Steve:	(Silence)

This chapter is about communication styles. In the story, Koh tries to show affection using words, and Shinji tries to be a good boyfriend by being silent, but their different styles lead to communication problems. Koh interprets Shinji's silence as disinterest, and Shinji thinks Koh is complaining, while she tells her friend she is simply explaining her feelings.

Communication gaps like these can be a problem between men and women, since male communication patterns and female communication patterns are often different. We can easily think that our intentions and ideas are obvious, while they are not. When dealing with someone from a different culture we have to pay special attention to minimize misunderstanding.

Communication style refers to the way we use different strategies to communicate. In all languages, people give compliments, agree and disagree, praise, ask for favors, make requests, seek clarification, show that they are listening, etc. The way these things are done, however, depends on the culture.

> Communication style refers to the way we use different strategies to communicate.

A commonly recognized difference in communication styles within Japan is that between Kansai and Kanto Japanese. It's not only the words that are different, it's the style of interaction. Also, older people and younger people often have different communication styles. Young people may seem too casual for the older generation. Comparing certain elements of English and Japanese strategies provides clear examples of different communication styles. In particular, there are differences in **directness**, **use of silence** and **cognitive styles**.

English speakers tend to be more direct than Japanese speakers. In a conflict between two residents of the same apartment complex, for example, English speakers are much more likely to go directly to the other resident to discuss the problem. Japanese speakers are more likely to use a go-between—the manager, for example—to avoid direct confrontation. To English speakers, this may seem sneaky or dishonest, while Americans may seem overly confrontational or blunt to Japanese. During business negotiations, English speakers (perhaps Americans in particular) often prefer to "put their cards on the table", or state their positions clearly. Japanese speakers are more likely to feel out the other's position indirectly.

In business settings, these differences can create serious problems not only when negotiating, but also with employee relations, or when dealing with customers.

Related to this is the use of silence. English speakers tend to be more verbal than Japanese speakers, emphasizing the speaker's choice of words and counting on that to carry the meaning accurately. Japanese speakers use silence more, emphasizing the context, and the listener's ability to fill in that which isn't said directly. The Japanese expression "listen one and understand ten" highlights that tendency in Japanese while the English expression "say what you mean and mean what you say" highlights English speakers' communication style.

> Listen one and understand ten.

> Say what you mean and mean what you say.

Another important difference between English and Japanese communication styles relates to the preferred cognitive style. English reasoning tends to be linear, beginning with the main point and then followed by supporting statements. Japanese reasoning is said to be circular, starting with background information, with the main point coming at the end.

Communication styles are a reflection of basic cultural values. It's possible to relate Japanese values towards indirectness and the use of intermediaries to the cultural values of saving face and emphasizing harmonious relationships. Americans' more direct style of negotiating and expressing opinions can be tied to values placed on independence, for example.

No communication style can be said to be better than any other, and because these styles are tied so deeply to culture, it's not easy to change them. Understanding them better, however, allows us to choose a wider range of strategies to fit the situation that we are in.

Learning to use different communication strategies helps us better understand the point of view of others and be understood better. When learning a foreign language in distant lands, we need this adaptive skill. It's also important in our daily lives. It can help us to avoid unnecessary problems with friends and colleagues, whether we're involved in negotiations with a foreign business person, or, like Shinji in the restaurant, deeply involved in a discussion with a very important someone.

Did you know?

Some researchers categorize different cultures by degrees of **masculinity** and **femininity**. Masculine cultures value traits such as assertiveness, competition and material success. Cultures considered feminine value traits such as quality of life, interpersonal relationships and concern for the weak. Male cultures emphasize differences between men and women, whereas feminine cultures allow for more overlapping between male and female roles.

Some highly male-oriented cultures: Japan, Austria, Venezuela, Italy, Switzerland, Mexico, Ireland, Great Britain, Germany

Some highly female-oriented cultures: Sweden, Norway, the Netherlands, Denmark, Finland, Chile, Portugal, Thailand

(Adapted from *Intercultural Communication*, Fred Jandt, Sage Publication, 1995)

8 : Communication Styles (1)

Focus on Content

1. According to the text, we can find differences in communication styles between:
   a. Kansai and Kanto.
   b. Men and women.
   c. English and Japanese.
   d. all of the above

2. According to the text, English is different from Japanese in the use of:
   a. directness.
   b. silence.
   c. cognitive style.
   d. all of the above

3. According to the text, communication styles:
   a. are related to the kind of strategies we use when communicating.
   b. are something we choose to show our personality.
   c. are only a problem between people of different countries.
   d. are the same all over the world.

4. According to the text, Japanese communication:
   a. emphasizes words more than English.
   b. emphasizes the speaker's responsibility for communication.
   c. emphasizes context more than English.
   d. emphasizes silence less than English.

5. According to the text, Americans might feel Japanese are sneaky because:
   a. Americans are overly confrontational.
   b. Japanese are often very direct.
   c. of Japanese indirect conflict resolution strategies.
   d. of American indirect conflict resolution strategies.

Culture Quiz

Test your cultural intuition about male-female communication in the U.S.

According to research done in classrooms, homes, business offices and hospitals, are the following statements true or false?

1. Men talk more than women. T / F
2. Women are more likely to touch each other than men. T / F
3. Women use less personal space than men. T / F
4. Men interrupt women more than they interrupt other men. T / F
5. Women are more likely to give information on intimate personal matters than men. T / F

(This quiz was adapted from *Intercultural Communication*, Fred Jandt, Sage Publications, 1995)

Activities

1. **Think** about the communication styles of a male and female you know very well, like your mother and father, or sister and brother. What differences in communication style do they have? What differences are primarily because of gender?

2. In pairs, **pantomime** a conversation between two women of your own age, then one between two men. Then a woman with a man. How did you feel? What did you notice?

3. Work with a partner. One person should try to pantomime the following tasks either "as a man" or "as a woman" without telling his/her partner which. The partner should **guess** whether the pantomime is "male" or "female".

bow	eat a bowl of noodles
shake hands	take a drink
talk on the phone	brush/comb one's hair
laugh	sit
tell a story	stand

4. Try to **think** of actions that don't change regardless of whether a man or woman does them.

Chapter 9
Communication Styles (2)

The Osaka Uncle

Katsuyoshi's company recently transferred him to New York. In a letter to an American friend he talks about how his experience as a young boy was similar to what he is now going through.

I grew up in my grandmother's hilltop home in Nagano. The household was proper, established and orderly, but with gentle warmth. Certain things could not be touched, certain subjects not discussed. Within those bounds I was pampered. To wander outside of them was unthinkable.

My uncle sometimes came from Osaka on business. His presence always excited me. He expected me to be a boy, wrestle before dinner, and burp when grandma went for more tea. I loved him and was envious of his children. He regularly invited me to his house but Grandma always gently put him off, and every time he left, his legend grew inside me.

In the summer when I was twelve, I threw a tantrum the day after my uncle's visit. That same afternoon, grandma reserved me a ticket for Osaka. I was ecstatic. My uncle wasn't home when I arrived. I was shown where to put my things, given a tour and introductions, then left to fend for myself until dinner. My cousins and their friends gathered around and looked me over, curious and excited. I was intimidated. They asked me about school and the games I played, but got impatient with my careful answers. They invited me to play baseball but I said I didn't know how.

My uncle came home and greeted me with rough enthusiasm. I grinned with expectation but was disappointed that after a while he settled down with his newspaper and a beer. My cousins came to him and competed for his attention, explaining the day's triumphs while he only half listened.

During my whole visit I felt uncertain and off-balance. I never knew what to do or say. I was expected to give my opinions and complain if something didn't suit me. That didn't mean, however, that anyone would do anything for me. A level of individualism and independence was required of me that I wasn't used to. The rules of the house were less clear and more negotiated, but since I was used to being with people who anticipated my needs, I felt left out.

Now, I find myself in New York feeling the same thing all over. My colleagues ask questions like, "So, what do you feel like eating?" even though I don't know the restaurants. In meetings, no one pauses long enough for me to speak. People cut each other off during discussions and I get left behind. Talking seems more important than listening. Also, I feel that I don't know the people I work with well enough to communicate well. I like working in New York, but it is going to take time to get used to it.

2-8   There are parallels with Katsuyoshi's life in Japan and in his grandmother's home, and his life in New York and in his uncle's home in Osaka. Japanese society, like his home in Nagano, tends to emphasize predictability and particular behavior in particular situations. U.S. culture, like his uncle's house, tends rather to place emphasis on spontaneity and self-assertion. These tendencies can be described as deep-rooted differences in communication patterns.

What Katsuyoshi is feeling is related to **communication context**. Context is the shared information that two communicators rely on as background for their messages. Communicators who share a lot of knowledge about each other, like two family members, can communicate very efficiently, because they have so much shared background. A few words can communicate a lot, as when a child shows a pair of torn pants to his or her mother, and she says, "Oh no, not again!" The mother doesn't need to say, "Oh no, you tore your pants last week, and now you've torn them again this week. I wasn't happy about it then, and now I'm even less happy." Most of the message that the mother is trying to communicate is contained within the shared knowledge of her and her child. This kind of communication is sometimes called "high context communication".

Oh no, not again!

When two communicators don't share much information, like when people meet for the first time at a party, they have to rely on words more to communicate. This "low context communication" cannot assume that the other communicator will easily grasp meaning, so messages tend to be more concrete and detailed to leave less room for misinterpretation. Lawyers who argue cases in a courtroom need to be very explicit and detailed in their communication, because often the jury, for example, only knows about the case from what they hear. They have no shared experience of the people and places involved.

Different cultures can also be compared by how much people tend to rely on shared information in their communication. Japan is a relatively **high context culture**, while the U.S. is a relatively **low**

Expressions like *haragei* show that Japanese culture emphasizes an appreciation of context.

context culture. Expressions like *haragei* show that Japanese culture emphasizes an appreciation of context and the ability to understand without relying on words. In English, expressions like "to give one's word" or "tell it like it is" show an emphasis on the use of words themselves to carry the bulk of the meaning.

Another way to compare cultures and their communication styles is high vs. low involvement. Involvement is a measure of outward expressiveness when interacting with others. To Japanese, who have a relatively low involvement culture, **high involvement cultures**, like many in the Middle East or Latin America, may seem highly emotional and expressive, using more body language and having a highly interactive style of communication.

These differences in communication patterns create some of the most difficult barriers for communicating well in foreign languages. These patterns are deeply rooted and can't be changed easily, but they can be understood. Recognizing that our communication style comes from our culture can help us to get beyond stereotypes, like "Japanese are shy", or "Americans are friendly". Our communication style is a product of not only our personality but also our environment. Let's hope that the author of the story finds a way to adapt to his new environment. If he does, he may be able to enjoy spontaneous New York, as he did the visits of his rough-and-tumble uncle from Osaka.

Did you know?

The style of giving opinions in English and Japanese is opposite. In **Japanese**, an opinion is the end product of a discussion or deliberation which attempts to take into account the point of view of all those involved. An opinion requires great effort to produce and only takes form at the end of discussion or deliberations. In **English**, on the other hand, an opinion is often used as the first step in examining the merits of different alternatives. One person gives a personal opinion which is then agreed with or questioned, defended, then strengthened or discarded. As the discussion or deliberation goes on, more opinions come out and are compared. Ideally, the debate of the different options produces a majority view about the best option. A dissenting view often still exists even after a decision has been made. In this sense, in English, an opinion is a starting point, not an end point.

Focus on Content

1. According to the text, context means:
   a. information shared by two communicators.
   b. coming from the same country as the other communicator.
   c. a communication technique used in English.
   d. a way to rely more on words to communicate.

2. The text finds parallels between:
   a. Nagano and Osaka.
   b. Nagano and New York.
   c. for Katsuyoshi, going to New York and going to Osaka as a child.
   d. for Katsuyoshi, living in NY and living in his grandmother's house.

3. In high context communication:
   a. most of the message is contained within the words.
   b. most of the message is contained within the shared context.
   c. words are not necessary at all.
   d. words are especially necessary.

4. According to the text, words like *haragei* reflect that Japan
   a. depends on words a lot.
   b. doesn't use words to communicate.
   c. values high context communication.
   d. values low context communication.

5. According to the text, Japan has a low involvement culture. This means:
   a. Japanese have few feelings.
   b. Japanese are very emotional.
   c. Japanese are less outwardly expressive than many cultures.
   d. Japanese are more outwardly expressive than many cultures.

Culture Quiz

Test your cultural intuition about communication styles around the world.

Choose which one of the two countries in each pair is regarded as having a higher context communication style.
1. U. S. A. - Germany
2. China - Sweden
3. Korea - England

Choose which one of the two countries in each pair is regarded as having a higher involvement communication style.
1. Korea - Japan
2. Mexico - U. S. A.
3. Saudi Arabia - Denmark

Activities

Work with a partner. **Tell** him or her a story about a person in one of the pictures on the next page. First, tell your story while your partner does not look at the picture, but just listens. Then, tell the story while your partner looks at the picture that you are talking about. **Discuss** whether looking at the picture together (sharing more information) made the story easier to understand, more interesting, etc.

DIFFERENT REALITIES

photograph A

photograph B

Chapter 10
Values

The Decision

Shinichiro received a terrible phone call in his university dormitory room. His father was sick. He left immediately for Kyushu. A week later he was back at school, and although he said his father was better, Shinichiro was silent and grim. He showed up unexpectedly at his girlfriend Hiroko's house one evening soon after that. Hiroko's friend Lisa, an Australian exchange student, happened to be there. Shinichiro sat quietly for a long time.

Lisa: Shin, you look terrible. Is it about your father?

Shin: He had a heart attack, but he's better now.

Lisa: That's good. (Pause)

Shin: The doctor said he can't work. He owns a cement factory. I have to quit school.

Lisa: What? Why? Your father said that?

DIFFERENT REALITIES

Shin: No, he didn't say anything, but my mother can't manage the business alone. I'm the only son. My uncle told me that everyone was counting on me to help for just a couple of years. Then I can come back to school if I want.

Lisa: Wow! What do you want to do?

Shin: (Long pause) I hate cement. I always dreamed of escaping that country town. I can't stand it there.

Lisa: What would happen if you didn't go?

Shin: Other relatives would help, but my mother would suffer a lot.

Lisa: Can't you go for just six months or a year?

Shin: I'd be trapped. Actually, my mother told me to stay in school, not to give up my dreams. She said that she would be all right.

Lisa: Well, that's good. I'm sure if you explain your feelings to your relatives they will understand. They can't expect you to give up everything here just because you are the only son.

Shin: (Long pause) I have to go back. That's my fate.

Later, after Shin had left, Lisa spoke with Hiroko.

Hiroko: What's wrong, Lisa?

Lisa: Oh, I'm so angry about Shin. What's wrong with him? How can he be so weak?

Hiroko: No (starting to cry), I think he's very strong... but it makes me very sad.

2-11 Life is full of choices big and small. Shin has to choose between maintaining his independence and his responsibility towards his family. His decision is based on his **values**. This chapter looks at what values are, and argues that to understand people from other cultures, we have to look at where our values come from, and how they might be different from those of people from other cultures.

Shin's feelings about what is important are his **personal values**. Even if he never consciously thinks about it, he still has ideas about what is right and wrong, fair or unreasonable, who deserves respect, how to be a good person, etc. In this case, his values tell him that responsibility towards his family is more important than continuing school.

Personal values reflect our personality. At the same time, our values do not come completely from our individual personality. As we grow up, we learn **cultural values**. We don't learn these values as rules, per se, but indirectly from our family, neighbors, teachers, television, books, as well as through the way we are treated and what is expected of us, etc. In Japan, things like deferring to someone older than we are, the importance of cooperation, the importance of trying hard, are important cultural values. This doesn't mean that everyone always lives up to these standards, but simply that they are important to keep in mind when deciding things.

> As we grow up, we learn cultural values.

Most people never think about how their values depend on their culture. Many may assume that humans are fundamentally the same, and that therefore, basic human values are also the same. It's not that simple, however. There are many things that people in all cultures do—they are born, raised and educated; they eat food, make friends, have families, maintain a place to live, show their emotions, have disagreements, and are mourned after death. But the normal or acceptable way to do all of these things depends on culture.

Differences in cultural values are very obvious in customs and traditional social institutions. Some form of marriage is common to all cultures, but practices vary widely. In some cultures, to get married and have children at age 17 or 18 is considered usual. Some

> In some cultures, to get married and have children at age 17 or 18 is considered usual.

cultures, including Korean and many in the Middle East and Latin America, consider a woman's virginity until marriage very important. Japanese values towards marriage may seem to people from some cultures quite liberal, conservative or even strange, because people in those cultures have different values.

Differences in cultural values are also easy to see when we compare how people make decisions about their lives. At what age should children stop living with their parents? Should women work? How should one best raise children? How important is it to be independent? How much responsibility does one have towards one's family? What is the role of religion in life? What happens after death? What is success? What is the purpose of life?

A culture's values are reflected in its proverbs. An often cited example from Japan is "The nail that sticks out gets hammered down". There is no equivalent expression in English. On the other hand, there is no exact Japanese equivalent to "God helps those who help themselves". This expression emphasizes individual self-reliance, and reflects the religious roots of western English-speaking culture.

> God helps those who help themselves.

As stated before, values do not cause people to act in a certain way; rather, they are the ideals that cultures judge by. Sometimes two different values are in conflict. An employee who discovers a colleague breaking the law may agonize about whether to report it or not. Shin also faced this kind of value dilemma with his decision about his family.

In intercultural situations differences in values can cause serious problems. A business started in a foreign country can fail because managers don't understand the values and customs of their local employees. Visitors to foreign countries can have negative impressions about those countries because people seem immoral, or rude, or irresponsible, simply because of cultural difference. These impressions can reinforce negative stereotypes and make people less tolerant even as they gain intercultural experience.

Values are more than abstractions found in an intercultural communication textbook. As with Shin's decision about his family, they are deeply felt issues related to all aspects of our lives and our happiness. As we dig deeper into culture, we may find that understanding value differences is the most important element in learning about ourselves and appreciating people from different cultures—even if we never manage a business abroad, or need to choose between our dreams and a cement factory.

Did you know? 2-12

When the Spanish conquerors arrived in what is now Mexico, they were helped by the fact that the Aztecs, the ruling group of indigenous people, had a legend which stated that a white-skinned god would appear from the East and come to rule over the Aztecs. In addition, because they had never seen horses before, seeing the Spaniards in their armor on horses may have given the Aztecs the impression that the Spaniards were strange, god-like creatures. The Aztecs soon realized their mistake, but in the end these misunderstandings may have contributed to the fall of the Aztec empire.

Focus on Content

1. According to the text, personal values:
   a. control our actions.
   b. are completely personal.
   c. depend to some degree on our personality.
   d. are the same as those of other people in our culture.

2. According to the text, values:
   a. are fundamentally the same everywhere.
   b. depend completely on one's culture.
   c. are not related to things that people everywhere do.
   d. reflect ideas about the right way to do things.

3. According to the text, values about cultural universals like marriage:
   a. are similar everywhere because all humans do those things.
   b. vary widely regarding how best to do those things.
   c. show us that human behavior should be judged by a single standard.
   d. are obvious enough to make deciding correct values easy.

4. According to the text, proverbs:
   a. show universal human wisdom.
   b. reflect what is felt to be important in a particular culture.
   c. can usually be easily translated.
   d. reflect religious ideas.

5. According to the ideas in the text, Shinichiro is facing difficulties related to:
   a. his personal values, which are related to his cultural values.
   b. his personal values, which are not related to his cultural values.
   c. his cultural values, which are not related to his personal values.
   d. none of the above

10 : Values

Culture Quiz

Test your cultural intuition about values and customs.

1. In Japan, children are sometimes punished by being left outside of their home. In the United States, a typical punishment is:
    a. leaving the child outside.
    b. not allowing the child to go outside.
    c. tying children's hands behind their back.
    d. having the child sit on his/her hands.

2. In Latin America, there is a customary celebration of reaching the age of dating and marriage. This takes place when a young woman reaches what age?
    a. 15   b. 17   c. 19   d. 21

3. In Thailand, Buddhist monks (men) receive offerings of food in bowls which they carry around with them. When receiving an offering from a woman, they set the bowl on the ground. This is to:
    a. show that women's position is lower than men's.
    b. symbolize respect for the importance of maternity.
    c. respect the gentleness of women compared to men.
    d. avoid the possible temptation of physical contact with a woman.

4. In Ireland, the traditional gathering after someone dies:
    a. involves sitting for several hours in silence out of respect for the deceased.
    b. involves a party with an emphasis on enjoyment to overcome the sadness of death.
    c. involves many loud verbal prayers to help the deceased enter heaven.
    d. involves recounting memories so that the deceased will always be remembered.

5. In Muslim and Jewish culture, pork is not eaten because:
    a. it is associated with non-believers.
    b. it is believed to be unhealthy.
    c. it is considered unclean.
    d. it is considered sacred.

DIFFERENT REALITIES

Activities

1. **Discuss** what you would do in Shin's position.

2. Below are some proverbs in English. See if you can **find** what cultural values are represented by them. See if you can find equivalent expressions in Japanese.

    A penny saved is a penny earned.
    Pull oneself up by one's bootstraps.
    A rolling stone gathers no moss.
    Do to others as you would have them do to you.
    Don't look a gift horse in the mouth.

    Below are some proverbs translated from Spanish. Try the same as you did above with them.

    Don't look for three legs on a cat.
    Lantern in the street, and candle at home.
    The shrimp that sleeps gets carried off by the current.
    It is not the same to talk of bulls as to be in the bullring.

    Make a list of Japanese proverbs. Choose the ones you think might help non-Japanese understand Japan.

3. **Imagine** you are explaining Japanese values about marriage and raising children to someone from a different country. Consider the following questions. What is an appropriate age for marriage in Japan? Why not younger, or older? How much difference in age between the man and woman is considered normal? What is the most important thing to keep in mind when raising children? How should children be disciplined?

4. **Compare** your personal values about some of the following topics with classmates, parents, teachers, etc.
    importance of schooling
    meaning of success
    living together before marriage
    entering a company immediately after graduation from university

Chapter 11
Deep Culture (Beliefs and Values)

"Doctor, what should I do? My husband has started believing in some weird Eastern philosophy..."

"Master, what should I do? My wife has started believing in some weird Freudian psychology..."

The Mystery of Antonio

2-13

Eriko was confused and upset. She quietly excused herself from the living room of her homestay family, went into her bedroom and tried not to cry. It was after 7:00. Her party was supposed to start at 6:00, but still not a single one of her new friends from her high school had arrived. In addition, that same day she had been laughed at by a large group of classmates, and wasn't sure why. She had been talking about her party—her friends seemed excited—and she had mentioned that she had invited Antonio. One girl then said she shouldn't have invited him, and another said that he wouldn't come anyway. Now Eriko wondered if she had done something wrong and that now no one was coming.

Her first impression of Mexico City had been somewhat shocking, but very interesting. The streets seemed especially wild at first, with street vendors selling food, people coming and going, children selling gum and sometimes even beggars asking for money. Her homestay family's home was nicer than she expected, much nicer than her home in Japan. It was large, with a three-car garage and a satellite-dish antenna. Every day she walked down a hill to her school, a private all-girls school with a large athletic ground and swimming pool.

In front of the gates of the school were several street stands that sold food to the students. One of them sold paper cups full of pieces of mango, papaya, orange and banana. Antonio ran this stall and Eriko thought him good-looking, with dark skin and a strong face. He was about the same age as the girls and joked with them when he sold fruit. Though he seemed friendly, the girls ignored him. Eriko sometimes stayed to talk with him because it was good practice for her Spanish, and because he was attractive.

Now Eriko wondered if there was some dark terrible secret about Antonio that no one had mentioned. When she had invited him to the party he seemed to be confused, or surprised. It had occurred to Eriko that maybe in Mexico girls shouldn't invite boys to parties. Still, she couldn't understand why her friends would decide not to come. As she was wondering about all of this, and wishing she were back in Japan, she heard the doorbell ring.

2-14 Eriko is upset because of cultural misunderstanding. Her friends laughed at her inviting Antonio because he is from a different social class. He is a street vendor, almost certainly from a working-class family, whose education and upbringing are entirely different than that of the girls at Eriko's private (probably expensive) school. Also, her friends' use of time is different. For them, a house party that is scheduled for five will probably only really get going at six or seven, and so they are showing up accordingly. Everyone knows these expectations and so no one is disappointed or surprised (except Eriko).

Eriko's misunderstanding comes from differences in **deep culture**. Deep culture is the most fundamental beliefs and values of a group of people. It is related to things like time, social status, beliefs about human nature, the purpose of human existence and many other abstract concepts.

To understand deep culture, one has to understand beliefs. **Beliefs** are the things which a person or a culture accept as true. An obvious example is religious beliefs—that God exists, for example. Less obvious are unconscious beliefs, like that life is fundamentally controlled by fate, or that humans can control nature, or that logic yields truth. **Values** are based on beliefs, and represent what is thought to be right or wrong. The value that stealing is wrong rests on the acceptance of a belief in ownership. When Europeans first came to North America, they found native peoples who believed that humans are an extension of nature, and so the concept of owning or buying land had no meaning.

The beliefs and values of deep culture are usually so much taken for granted that they can be difficult to even discuss. **Use of time** is one example. In Japanese culture (as well as North American, German and others), time is seen as a part of objective reality; something which can be measured, saved and wasted. It is natural then that human activity is controlled to a great degree by time. "Please be on time for the meeting; we have to finish the project by tomorrow."

> Time is used like any other resource to organize life efficiently and improve the quality of human existence.

Some other cultures, like many Latin American and Middle Eastern cultures, see time quite differently. Humans are assumed to possess a spiritual nature which sets us apart from animals and our mere physical environment. To force humans to be controlled too much by time brings us down to the level of machines, and at-

> To force humans to be controlled too much by time brings us down to the level of machines.

tacks human dignity. It isn't that Japanese don't think that humans have a spiritual nature, or that Latins don't use time to live efficiently, but that there is a difference in degree. While most people don't talk about the nature of time, we can see by looking at how different cultures use the concept of time that there are important fundamental differences.

Another important element of deep culture is beliefs and values about **individualism** versus **collectivism**. Some cultures, like in Australia and North America, stress individual identity, emphasizing those things which make one unique. Collectivistic cultures put greater emphasis on an individual's relationship with the people in the groups he/she belongs to. Researchers estimate that around 70% of the world's population belongs to collectivistic cultures. Mexico, for example, is considered a collectivistic culture, although group identity is more related to family and social background than in Japan.

Every culture has ways to show differences in social status. The president of a large company has more status than a clerical worker; movie stars have more than construction workers, etc. This **power distance** is dealt with differently, however, in different cultures. High power distance cultures, like Japan's, show differences in status in obvious ways, like titles, and through the use of honorific language. Low power distance cultures, like in the United States, value making status invisible. Status difference still exists, but it is considered impolite to make open reference to it.

This does not mean that low power distance cultures are more equal; it means that status is dealt with differently. Japan has a high power distance culture, yet has a very egalitarian distribution of wealth by world standards. The United States has a low power distance culture, but has significant and persistent differences in wealth among different parts of society.

Deep culture is quite a difficult concept to talk about. Also, comparing our most basic values and beliefs with those of other cultures may involve difficult questions of identity. Eriko may feel that treating Antonio differently because of social position is unfair, just as people from some cultures might find it offensive that Japanese show status differences with honorific language. Understanding others' values, though, teaches us about ourselves and helps us appreciate people from other cultures—even if their beliefs seem strange, or they don't come to our parties when we expect them to!

Did you know?

The concept of social class can easily be misunderstood. In cultures where class identity is strong, belonging to a certain class is not necessarily related to income. A successful business owner from a working-class background may be rich, but most likely will not identify strongly with people who are considered upper class in that culture. On the other hand, a family which has an upper-class background and values may have less money than the business owner. In class-oriented cultures, people often talk of class in terms of one's education. However, what it means to be **educated** may be different depending on class. In Latin America, class distinctions are relatively strong. A Mexican and a Venezuelan from the same social class may feel closer than two Mexicans from different social classes.

Focus on Content

1. According to the text, Eriko's friends laughed at her because:
   a. in Mexico girls don't invite boys to parties.
   b. she planned to start the party too early.
   c. Antonio doesn't go to that school.
   d. Antonio is of a different social class.

2. According to the text, deep culture is:
   a. the oldest part of a culture.
   b. feelings about what is true and important.
   c. traditional customs.
   d. the most talked about cultural beliefs and values.

3. According to the text, Japanese culture sees time:
   a. similar to North Americans.
   b. similar to Latin Americans.
   c. different from most other cultures.
   d. the same as most other cultures.

4. According to the text, collectivistic cultures:
   a. are relatively rare in the world.
   b. emphasize how one individual is different from another.
   c. put importance on relationships in groups.
   d. have strong social class distinctions.

5. According to the text, cultures with low power distance:
   a. are generally less equal than high power distance cultures.
   b. find open discussion of social status impolite.
   c. show differences in social status openly.
   d. don't have different social classes.

11 : Deep Culture (Beliefs and Values)

Culture Quiz

Test your understanding about some fundamental beliefs.

1. Science is based on the belief that:
    a. finding truth depends on human experience.
    b. objective truths exist independently of human belief.
    c. truth depends on one's point of view.
    d. no absolute truths exist.

2. Generally, Christians believe that Jesus:
    a. was a man who communicated directly with God.
    b. was God in a man's body.
    c. was purely a spirit.
    d. was a wise man who taught virtues.

3. The most fundamental belief of Buddhism is that:
    a. human nature is sinful.
    b. one should try to live like the Buddha.
    c. life's suffering is caused by illusion.
    d. meditation helps us communicate with God.

4. The traditional Chinese philosophy of Taoism is based on the belief that:
    a. the world is in harmony.
    b. the world is not in harmony.
    c. good is equal in power to evil.
    d. the universe consists of a balance of opposing forces.

5. One fundamental belief of modern physics theory is that:
    a. time is not absolute.
    b. matter and energy are fundamentally different.
    c. light is not affected by gravity.
    d. energy can be created.

DIFFERENT REALITIES

Activities

A. Below is a list of beliefs from around the world. Which of these do you agree with personally? **Mark** (a) if you agree strongly, (b) if you agree, (c) if you neither agree or disagree, (d) if you disagree, and (e) if you disagree strongly. **Compare** your answers to others. Where do these beliefs come from?

1. Progress is important.   a b c d e
2. History gives life meaning.   a b c d e
3. Work and play are different.   a b c d e
4. One's individual values determine one's identity.   a b c d e
5. Money is an important measure of success.   a b c d e
6. The earth is alive.   a b c d e
7. The world is full of mysterious forces.   a b c d e
8. Only God can determine what is right and wrong.   a b c d e
9. Only by being objective can we find truth.   a b c d e
10. Some special people can communicate with spirits.   a b c d e
11. Science improves our lives.   a b c d e
12. Dead ancestors can influence us.   a b c d e
13. One's fate cannot be changed.   a b c d e
14. After death we are born again into a different body.   a b c d e
15. After death we go to heaven or hell.   a b c d e
16. Humans can become enlightened.   a b c d e
17. Life was better in the past.   a b c d e
18. People are fundamentally evil.   a b c d e
19. My culture is unique.   a b c d e

B. Choose items from above that you think are important and fundamental values and beliefs in Japanese culture. Compare your list with others.

Chapter 12
Culture Shock

Fred and Mildred, after visiting 36 temples on their four-day visit to Japan, suddenly go into culture shock.

Going Home 2-16

Matt is an American from a small town in Oregon. He recently arrived in Niigata and started working as an assistant English teacher in a rural high school. He is having difficulty adjusting to his new life. The following is an e-mail message which he wrote to a friend back in the U.S.

Dear Jeremy,

Thanks for your message. Yes, Japan is a fascinating country, but I've been pretty depressed lately. I've only been here three months but I may not finish my contract.

The first month was great. I wrote you about the rice fields around where I live, and the vending machines that sell hot canned drinks. Everything was interesting. Even now it's weird to have students bow when the teacher comes into class, and I still look the wrong way before crossing the street.

The phones are cool too. You use a magnetic debit card and there's a digital readout telling you how many units you have left.

It's gotten old though. After a while I started getting tired of feeling like a total idiot 99 percent of the time. I needed help with everything—opening a bank account, buying train tickets, understanding menus . . . I even bought mayonnaise (it comes in a plastic tube) thinking it was hand cream. There seems to be nothing that is completely the same as at home—except McDonalds! Of course even then I have trouble ordering and it's really expensive.

I guess things aren't that bad now though. I've gotten my routine down so things aren't so confusing anymore. I'm not sure why I've been so depressed recently, though I do miss my friends. I don't have anyone here I can really relax around and I'm the only foreigner in the area. Also, things which were interesting at first are starting to get on my nerves. Every day at the cafeteria at my school I nearly scream because the food never changes—miso soup, rice and something else which is often cold or weird.

I know I shouldn't complain. Everyone here has been really nice to me, even though it seems phony sometimes. Maybe I'm just lonely. Recently I sleep a lot and I'm irritable. After work and on weekends I stay home and watch videos. I've been eating a lot of cup-ramen and scrambled eggs. I really miss those nights with you eating pizza (they have tuna and corn on pizza here!) and channel surfing. My TV here only has about five channels.

Well, I'll give it a bit more time, but I don't expect things to get better. It sucks to think I came all this way just to be miserable and depressed. I hope I pull out of it soon. If not, you may see me home sooner than you expected.

Matt

2-17 Matt is feeling stress because he hasn't been able to adjust to all of the newness of his surroundings yet. He's irritable, sleeps a lot and doesn't go out. He's frustrated by the food, the difficulty of doing things and his relationships with people. He is even considering going back to the United States. It might help Matt if he knew that almost everyone who goes to live in a different country suffers from similar trouble. The feeling, **culture shock**, is the unavoidable stress related to adapting to a new cultural environment.

> At home, our everyday lives are filled with familiar choices and routines.

At home, our everyday lives are filled with familiar choices and routines. We get up and our clothes are where they always are. Our breakfast is the same as on countless mornings. We go to school or work as usual. During the day we talk mostly to people we know, or people who do nothing that surprises us. In the evening we socialize in places where we understand the menu at a glance, can easily order and judge if the service or food is good or bad. Talking with friends is effortless. We go home using our usual means of transportation, wash ourselves in the usual way and go to sleep in a bed that is familiar. Even the choices we make are familiar. Should I buy an eight-slice loaf of bread or six? How much is the fare to the station I want to go to?

In a new environment all of these things change. The excitement of being in an exotic place changes to stress as the details of living require more mental and emotional energy than we have. We may sleep a lot, get bothered or emotional very easily. We may get homesick and think a lot about familiar people and places. People with little experience away from home, or who dislike changes in their routines, often have more trouble. Fortunately, most people get over culture shock and are able to adapt. Understanding the process and being ready for it when it happens is the

> People with little experience away from home, or who dislike changes in their routines, often have more trouble.

only solution.

We can think of the adaptation process in four steps. First is **culture surprise**, when everything looks fresh and exciting. Next is **culture stress**, when we start to be bothered by how difficult or strange or unfamiliar things are. Next is **culture shock**, which is a deeper, more upsetting stage than culture stress. In culture shock we are depressed or bothered or upset for what seems to be no particular reason. We may also have physical symptoms like insomnia or headaches. Culture shock comes from accumulated culture stress and may be mild or severe and can last a short or long time. The final stage is **culture adaptation**. As we adapt, we regain our sense of normal self, become more outgoing and regain our emotional balance.

Culture shock is unpleasant, but it and the adaptation process are completely natural. Reminding oneself that negative feelings may be related to culture shock and not expecting oneself to be perfectly comfortable immediately can help the transition. Having a sense of humor about one's new environment also helps.

One Japanese woman who went to the U.S. said that culture surprise started when she saw the size of the freeways after being picked up at the airport; that culture stress started with the welcoming hug of her homestay mother; and that she started the process of adapting two months later when she laughed uncontrollably after spilling a glass of milk while eating breakfast. She said the glass was three times as big as any at her home in Japan, and that somehow the flood of milk broke her tension.

> She started laughing uncontrollably after spilling a glass of milk while eating breakfast.

If Matt doesn't give up too soon, he will certainly start to feel better about his life in Japan. Living life under the control of the unconscious habits of our culture is a natural process, but it means that fully adapting to a different environment can be difficult and take time. Fortunately, learning is also a natural human process which Matt can count on to eventually help him adjust, even if that means eating corn and tuna on his pizza!

Did you know?

There are a number of steps one can take to make adjusting to a new environment easier. For example, before leaving home: **1 - Talk to people** who have been where you are going to find out the difficulties they had. **2 - Find out** as much about your new environment and living situation as possible. After arriving: **1 - Develop new routines** starting with your most immediate environment—your room and neighborhood—and then move outward from there to stores, transportation networks, etc. **2 - Seek out** people from your own country, getting advice and help. Be careful though; some of them may be having trouble adjusting and might be negative. **3 - Remember** that whatever difficult feelings you are having, they are natural and will pass as you get used to your new environment. Once that happens keep exploring and make the most of your experience. Before you know it, it will be time to go back.

Focus on Content

1. According to the text, culture shock is:
    a. an unpleasant emotion caused by newness.
    b. an enjoyable feeling of excitement about a new environment.
    c. the surprise of finding unusual things in a new environment.
    d. feeling bothered by not being able to do things.

2. According to the text, the routines of our everyday life at home:
    a. help prevent culture shock.
    b. are soon transferred to our new environment.
    c. aren't related to culture shock.
    d. cause new environments to be stressful.

3. According to the text:
    a. culture stress is more exciting than culture shock.
    b. culture shock causes culture stress.
    c. cultural stress builds up to cause culture shock.
    d. the specific causes of culture shock are hard to identify.

4. When Matt says that everything in Japan was interesting at first, he was feeling:
    a. culture surprise.
    b. culture stress.
    c. culture shock.
    d. culture adaptation.

5. According to the text, culture shock:
    a. cannot be prevented because it is unnatural.
    b. is gotten over by the natural process of adaptation.
    c. can be completely prevented by learning about the new environment.
    d. usually is not gotten over.

Culture Quiz

Below are some customs which might contribute to culture shock. Test your knowledge of the countries where these customs might be found.

1. People hold hands even with people they don't know well. If you ask for directions, a stranger might take your hand to lead you to your destination.
    a. Malaysia
    b. Sweden
    c. West Africa
    d. Peru

2. It's not unusual for people (especially women) to greet each other with a kiss on the cheek.
    a. the United States
    b. Turkey
    c. Singapore
    d. France

3. There is same-sex touching in public. You can see men with their arms around each other, or a man resting his head on the shoulder of another man on a train or bus, for example.
    a. Switzerland
    b. Australia
    c. Canada
    d. China

4. It is not unusual for a friend or acquaintance to drop by your house without calling or telling you beforehand.
    a. England
    b. the Middle East
    c. the U.S.
    d. Canada

5. It is not unusual for people to ask the price of something you own, or ask you what your salary is.
    a. Peru
    b. Kenya
    c. Singapore
    d. Korea

Activities

1. **Answer** the following questions to find out how routine your life is. **Compare** your answers with others.

   1. How many different things can you remember having for breakfast recently?
   2. When was the last time you slept somewhere for the first time?
   3. When was the last time you made a new friend?
   4. When did you last ask someone for directions?
   5. When did you last try a new food?
   6. Have you ever completely changed your hair style?
   7. How many times have you moved in your lifetime?

2. **Think** of a time when you found yourself in a new environment; for example, a new school or neighborhood. What problems did you have adjusting? What advice would you give to someone about to do the same?

3. **Choose** a foreign country that you know something about. Based on your knowledge of that country, what difficulties might you have if you moved there.

Notes

Chapter 1 Culture and Identity

1   キャプション **identical twins**「うりふたつの双子」
    4 **play practical jokes**「いたずらする」
2   3 **greasy**「脂っこい」
    13 **biology**「生物学上」ここでは同じ両親から生まれて血が繋がっているということ。
    22 **identity**「自己同一性」自分は何者であるかということ。自分の正体。
    23 **personality**「個々の性格；広義での個性」
3   15- **negative stereotypes**「否定的な固定概念〔イメージ〕」
    27 **Returnees**「帰国子女」
4   16 **interact with**「相互に作用する；互いに影響しあう」
    30- **integrating the disabled into society**「身体障害者を社会に融け込ませる」
5   10 **rewarding**「価値のある」
    10- **a fresh perspective on life**「人生の新しい見方」

Chapter 2 Hidden Culture

8   12 **vaguely**「漠然と」
9   7 **personal**「うちとけて」
    8- **impersonal**「距離を置いている；うちとけないさま」
    28 **not worth the trouble**「わざわざ苦労する価値がない」
10   1 **a flood of refugees**「大量の避難民〔亡命者〕」
    12 **to speak up**「言葉を発する；会話を始める」
    12- **in detail**「詳しく」
11   15 **small talk**「おしゃべり；ちょっとした会話；世間話」
    20 **the task at hand**「手近な任務；それに対して心の準備のできていること」
12   16 **outgoing**「社交的；外向的」

Chapter 3 Stereotypes

16   16 **upset**「うろたえる；当惑する」 日常会話のなかでは、怒る、いらいらするという意味で使われることが多い。
    24 **gender**「生物学的、肉体的な男女の性別(sex)に対して、歴史的、社会的な役割から生じた性別・性差」 シモーヌ・ド・ボーボワールの著作「第二の性」の一文「人は女に生まれるのではない。女になるのだ」はこのgenderに言及している。60

DIFFERENT REALITIES

年代以降のフェミニズムの台頭で、sex とは、明確に区別して使われる。
- 27- **indigenous peoples**「先住民；原住民」 例えば合衆国における Native American、日本のアイヌ民族、ニュージーランドのマオリ族など。

17 4 **habits of perception**「固定的な見方；癖になった見方」
- 10 **like weeds** 雑草のように、抜いても抜いても生えてくる執拗さ、粘り強さの比喩。
- 14 **pop up**「ひょいと顔を出す；飛び出す」

18 6 **sneaky**「こそこそと卑劣な；油断ならない」 1941年の旧日本海軍のハワイ真珠湾攻撃は、正式の宣戦布告の前であったことから、アメリカでは sneak attack と呼ばれている。またゴム底運動靴を sneakers と呼ぶのは、音を立てないでこっそり歩くことができるからであろう。
- 17 **to minimize**「最小限にする」
- 23 **workaholics**「仕事中毒」 *cf.* alcoholics
- 26 **objective**「客観的」
- 26- **subjective**「主観的」

19 13 **trapped by**「囚われる」
- 17 **to suspend judgment**「判断を先延ばしにする；差し控える」
- 26 **apartheid**「アパルトヘイト」 旧南ア連邦の悪名高い人種隔離政策。
- 27- **internment**「収容」＜ internment camp「(捕虜、敵性国人)収容所」 米国籍であるにも関わらず、多くの日系人が、第二次大戦下の1942年に議会を通過した強制疎開命令によって、僻地の収容所に送られた。
- 28 **massacre**「虐殺」

Chapter 4 Words, Words, Words

23 4 **excerpt**「(ここでは学校新聞の記事からの) 抜粋」
- 10 **carry**「持つ；伝える」
- 12 **a language exchange**「お互いの言語を教えあうこと」

24 6 **caring**「優しい；思いやりのある」
- 14 **in functional terms**「機能的な意味」 ここでは言葉を情報交換という機能の面だけで捉えること。
- 21 **equivalent**「同等の；同意義の」
- 25- **personal fulfillment**「自己実現；個人的な達成」

25 9 **Confucian ideas**「儒教的考え」 *cf.* Confucius「孔子(中国の思想家、儒教の始祖)」
- 10- **egalitarianism**「平等主義」
- 12 **in miniature**「縮小版での；小規模での」
- 20- **words create meaning that is already inside the listener**「言葉は、すでに聞き手の内にある意味を立ちあげる」
- 22- **the shared symbolic framework of the language**「人々が共有している記号としての言葉の枠組み」

26 14- **nigger, negro, Negro, Black and currently African American, or, as a**

broader category, persons of color nigger は黒人の蔑称で、差別が法によって保証されていた60年代の公民権運動以前は、かなり広く使われていた。現代でも差別主義者のあいだで使われるが、O.J. Simpson 裁判の際証人喚問されたマイク・ファーマン警部の昔のインタビュー・テープが、陪審員に公開され、その中で彼が nigger を連発していたことが、ロス市警に対する信頼を甚だしく失墜させたことは記憶に新しい。negro, Negro は、ラテン語 nigrum を語源とする、黒色を意味するスペイン語からの転用で、侮蔑的意味あいがある。Black は中立的表現としてもっとも一般的に使われるが、８０年代のPC（政治的適正論議）以来、個別文化性を強調する African American が使われるようになった。

27　14　**derogatory**「軽蔑的；侮蔑的」

Chapter 5　Communication Without Words

31　キャプション　**graffiti**「落書き」
32　5　**conceded**「（正しいと）認めた；しぶしぶ認めた」
　　16　**taken for granted**「当たり前のことと思う」
33　7　**unconscious**「無意識の」
　　16　**intuitively**「直感的に」
　　28　**comes down to**「詰まるところ～になる」
34　24　**stiff**「堅苦しい」
35　1　**insolent**「生意気；横柄」
　　9-　**the intricate dance of communication**「入り組んだ伝達のための動き」　dance は舞の連想から、身ぶり手振りを指すのに比喩的に使われた語。

Chapter 6　Diversity

40　2-　**the circumstances under which many thousands of Koreans came to Japan during the time of her grandparents**　1910年の日韓併合に始まる日本の朝鮮半島支配により、多くの韓国人が日本に連行され、行方が分からなくなった。ことに第二次大戦中の徴用目的の非人道的強制連行は、その後の謝罪の不完全さと相まって、いまだに国際世論の批判の対象となっている。
　　4-　**she couldn't escape them**「避けて通ることができなかった」
41　13-　**like-minded**「似たような考えを持つ」
　　14　**credit**「～に帰する；～のせいだと考える」
　　18　**an atmosphere of exclusion**「排他的雰囲気；除け者を作る雰囲気」
42　3　**Feeling sorry for**「可哀想に思う」
　　13　**commonality**「共通性」
43　3　**whose difference is invisible**「違いは見た目には分からない」

Chapter 7 Perception

47 3 **breaking up with**「別れる」
    7 **hug**「抱きしめる；抱擁する」
    7- **or anything**　ここでは何もしないことの強調。
48 22 **mind may already be made up**「考えがすでに決まっている」
   24 **off the point**「ずれている；文脈からはずれている」
49 2- **physical**「体で表す」
   11 **frowning**「顔をしかめる」
   29 **but different cultures divide the spectrum up in different ways**「文化によって色域（色の範囲）が異なる」
51 13- **artificial, and therefore, subservient concept**「人が作ったものであるゆえに、人が支配、左右できる概念」

Chapter 8 Communication Styles (1)

56 11 **crying and everything**「泣くやらなにやら」
57 5 **Gross**「汚い」
    9 **nosy**「何でも知りたがる；詮索好き」
   20 **Let's not start**「もう止めましょ」
58 21 **apartment complex**「アパートの棟」
   28- **put their cards on the table**「手の内を見せる」
   30 **feel out**「それとなく探る」
59 12- **say what you mean and mean what you say**「本当に思ったことを言い、その通りに行動する」
   17 **be linear**「直線的」
60 8 **a very important someone**「大切な人」　ここでは信二のガール・フレンドを指す。

Chapter 9 Communication Styles (2)

63 7 **pampered**「甘やかされた」
    9 **burp**「げっぷする」
64 1 **threw a tantrum**「かんしゃくを起こした」
    4 **to fend for myself**「自活する；独力でやる」　ここでは、かまわれず一人で過ごすの意。
   10 **settled down**「落ちついた；腰を落ちつけた」
65 23 **the jury**「陪審員」
66 4 **tell it like it is**「あるがままを言う」
    5 **the bulk of**「多くの」
   15 **are deeply rooted**「根深い」
   17 **to get beyond**「乗り越える」
   22 **rough-and-tumble**「無鉄砲な」

Chapter 10　Values

71　4　**grim**「厳めしい；しかめっ面」
72　11　**be trapped**「捕まる；動けなくなる」
73　13　**deferring**「譲る；従う」
　　16　**lives up to**「〜に従って行動する；実行する」
74　20　**God helps those who help themselves**「神は自ら助くるものを助ける」
75　12　**dig deeper**「深く入り込む」
　　18　**the Spanish conquerors**　中南米に栄えたアステカ帝国を1521年に滅ぼし、インカ帝国を1533年に滅亡させたコルテス、ピサロらを指す。
　　19　**the Aztecs**「アステカ人」　皇帝モクテスマ2世は、コルテスをアステカの神ケツァルコアトルの再来と信じて恭順したと言われる。
　　23　**armor**「鎧」

Chapter 11　Deep Culture (Beliefs and Values)

79　1　**excused herself from**「失礼した；その場から出た」
80　25　**only really get going**「実際に始まる」
81　20-　**to a great degree**「大いに；非常に」
82　3　**a difference in degree**「程度の差」
　　25　**to make open reference**「はっきりと言う」

Chapter 12　Culture Shock

87　7　**depressed**「憂鬱」
88　3　**It's gotten old though**「新鮮味がなくなる」
　　10　**I've gotten my routine down**「毎日のスケジュールに沿って行動する」
　　14　**to get on my nerves**「神経に障る」
　　18　**phony**「嘘っぽい」
　　23-　**It sucks**「むかつく；嫌気がさす」
　　25　**pull out of it**「抜け出す」
89　22　**get bothered**「いらいらする」
90　17　**help the transition**「移行を円滑にする」

著作権法上、無断複写・複製は禁じられています。

Different Realities　　　　　　　CD付　　　[B-565]
Adventures in Intercultural Communication
異文化間コミュニケーション —己を知る、相手を知る—

| 1 | 刷 | 2007年1月24日 |
| 20 | 刷 | 2025年2月28日 |

著　者　　ジョセフ・ショールズ　　Joseph Shaules
　　　　　阿部　珠理　　Juri Abe
　　　　　立教大学全学共通カリキュラム英語教育研究室

発行者　　南雲　一範　　Kazunori Nagumo

発行所　　株式会社　南雲堂
　　　　　〒162-0801　東京都新宿区山吹町361
　　　　　NAN'UN-DO Publishing Co., Ltd.
　　　　　361 Yamabuki-cho, Shinjuku-ku, Tokyo 162-0801, Japan
　　　　　振替口座：00160-0-46863
　　　　　TEL: 03-3268-2311(代表) / FAX: 03-3269-2486
　　　　　編集者　TA / YH

製版所　　MAGスタジオ

イラスト　伊丹　朋子

装　丁　　森山　隆

検　印　　省　略

コード　　ISBN978-4-523-17565-0　C0082

Printed in Japan

E-mail　nanundo@post.email.ne.jp
URL　https://www.nanun-do.co.jp/

┌─────────────────────────────────────┐
│　　　　文化の壁を超え、真の相互理解へ　　　　│
│　　　　　南雲堂の好評既刊書　　　　　│
└─────────────────────────────────────┘

見つめあう日本とアメリカ　異文化の新しい交差を求めて
　阿部珠理・御堂岡潔・渡辺信二編著

研究対象を日本とアメリカにしぼって文化相互の差異を明確にし、異文化交流の状況や障害となっている問題を検証。文学、言語、社会学の三分野の専門家が一つのテーマをもとに論文やエッセイを寄せ、異文化コミュニケーション論を展開する。

　　　　　　　　　　四六上製　252ページ　定価（本体2913円＋税）

沈黙のことば
　E.ホール／國弘正雄・長井善見・斉藤美津子共訳

話すことだけが唯一の伝達手段ではない、と非言語コミュニケーションの重要性を人類学者の立場から説いたコミュニケーション論の名著。普段は気にしない「沈黙のことば」の意味を探る。

　　　　　　　　　　四六並製　252ページ　定価（本体1942円＋税）

異文化を読む　　　岡部朗一著

日米間の経済摩擦・文化摩擦の底流に横たわる「ヒト」の摩擦に視点をすえ、コミュニケーション・ギャップを克服する新しい方法を模索する。

　　　　　　　　　　四六並製　256ページ　定価（本体2427円＋税）

日本語の意味　英語の意味　　　小島義郎著

日英の意味の比較を具体的・実践的に論じる。辞書には盛り込めないような問題も随所に入れ、日英両語の意味のずれを解きあかす。

　　　　　　　　　　四六上製　286ページ　定価（本体1942円＋税）

英米文化常識百科事典
　石黒昭博監修　山内信幸・南井正廣・北林利治共編

本辞典は英米文化を支えているものとして、何万という項目の中から日本人の英語学習者にとって英米文化の理解を深めるのに必要と思われる項目を精選。各項目をABC順に配列、高校生や大学生をはじめ英語教育に従事する先生や英語に興味をもつ社会人の要求に応えられるよう配慮した。

　　　　　　　　四六判ビニール装函入　438ページ　定価（本体4369円＋税）

┌───┐
│　〒162-0801　東京都新宿区山吹町361　Tel 03-3268-2311　│
└───┘